Yummy Raw Vegan Breakfast, Lunch, Dinn
GW00859487
Fat to
The Recipes that Inspired Pure Market Express
Written by Rebecca Irey
ARKET

Fat to Fit
The Recipes That Inspired Pure Market Express

v2.0

Outskirts Press, Inc.
http://www.outskirtspress.com

ISBN: 978-1-9772-2390-6

PRINTED IN THE UNITED STATES OF AMERICA

This book is dedicated to my husband,
Quentin, the best man I've ever known.
Thank you for loving my crazy!

And to each of my sweet children, who tolerated being plied
for months with new recipes and always smiled and said,
"It's good, Mama."
Even when it wasn't.
I love you all so very much.

Breakfast.........13

Crackers, Chips & Cereal.........23

Entrees.........32

Nuts to the Good Cheese.........59

Seriously Good Components.........69

Drinks.........73

Soup.........83

Desserts.........87

HOW I GOT FAT & HOW PIE CHANGED EVERYTHING

My name is Rebecca. This is the story of a cattle rancher's daughter turned raw vegan chef. This is my story. I was raised on a ranch in South Dakota. We raised crops and cattle. We ate meat and potatoes at every midday meal and usually every night as well, unless it was Saturday night when we always had pancakes and eggs.

If there was a vegetable at all, it was usually corn or green beans, boiled – isn't that the only way to make them? On holidays, we had salads with ranch dressing and potato salad or the ever-popular macaroni salad. My Aunt Sandy had a huge garden and would make me eat the cooked carrots or peas or beans which she loved. I did not love them. I would find a way to sneak to the garbage or to the bathroom to discard the detestable garden goodies so we could finally get to dessert.

I was very young when I met and married the love of my life. I did and still do feel exceptionally fortunate to have found the perfect man to cope with and even thrive on my special brand of crazy. I was pregnant with my first child at 18. I had heard you should eat for two – so I did – me and John Candy. I gained almost 100 pounds in that nine-month span and was blessed with a beautiful baby girl. I was never able to lose all of that weight - though I lost the same 50 - 60 pounds over and over again. And those same lost pounds somehow kept finding me again.

Quentin and I started our first business in healthcare in 1995. Over the next ten years, we had four more children (yes, that is 5!) and worked ridiculous hours to establish our business. In 2004, I was at my heaviest weight ever. The last weight I remember seeing at an OB appointment was almost 300 pounds. I was so depressed I drove through for ice cream on the way home - a lot of it. Deep down, I knew something had to give.

At a women's retreat, I was introduced to the raw food diet. Frankly, I thought it was the most ridiculous thing I had ever heard. When Quentin asked me what I learned when I got home, I plopped a bunch of bananas on the table and proclaimed, "Here's dinner!" But a seed was planted and when the woman who spoke at the retreat published a raw cookbook, I bought it.

I figured spaghetti would be an easy thing to whiz up so I bought a tiny spiralizer and set to work. I had never eaten a zucchini before so I decided to give it a whirl. Three hours later, I had a cold glop of thin stringy zucchini noodles coated in cold red goo that didn't taste any better than it looked. Failure. Abject and utter failure. Frustrated, I put the book on the shelf.

Six months later, I had to do a review for a long-time employee and good friend. I offered to take her out to lunch and asked what she might enjoy. She told me she really only liked to eat salads. Ugh. Okay, I thought, I'll take her to this restaurant I had heard about that only served raw vegan stuff. I could get through one meal with her and then go through the drive-through on the way home.

We ordered a "cheese" roll and a spicy "taco." I was nervous as the waitress set the meal before us. But I put my game face on and spread some of the cheese stuff on a cracker that looked like it might be just some kind of seed baked together? I tasted and was shocked. Before I knew what happened, every plate was empty. I loved it! THIS was vegetables? Where was the mushy corn and green beans? There were NO potatoes on the menu at all. I swear the taco had meat in it! It was fabulous and I was hooked. There was a book there called RAW by Juliano and it had a list of ingredients and supplies and I bought it on the spot.

I spent the weekend spending WAY too much on all the supplies recommended in the book and new gadgets galore. My poor husband! His wife was taken by the raw vegan body snatchers! I read the whole book and Amazon packages began to arrive in droves as I soaked in every bit of info I could get my hands on. I organized a lovely group of friends to come to the house once a month to make raw recipes with me so we could try some out together. (Kellee, Mona, Linda and Julie – love you guys!)

It seemed every book I read said you had to be 100% raw or it wasn't even worth trying. Cooked food was poison! No chemicals anywhere. Clean with slices of lemon, only coconut oil as a moisturizer and don't forget to swish your mouth with flax oil every morning to release toxins! Everyone around you is eating themselves to death. A Raw Monster was born. I announced I would not eat myself to death nor would I allow my children to. I would only "cook" raw. Being practical and considerate, I told my astonished (and have I mentioned saintly?) husband that he could eat that poison if he wanted to but he would have to make it himself. Oh Lord! I blush even as I type the words.

So the problem was the only two recipes I had really successfully made myself was a chocolate cheesecake that I almost chopped my finger off making trying to open a coconut with a cleaver – thank the Lord for electric tape, the great healer – and chocolate brownies made of walnuts and cacao. Everything else, even the raccoons who religiously scavenged our garbage, wouldn't eat.

But if not 100% then it wasn't worth it soooo I committed that I would eat whatever I wanted, whenever I wanted as long as it was raw. For six months, the Raw Monster ruled my home and I lived mostly on chocolate cheesecake and learned to make pastas, lasagnas, cookies, wicked good salad dressings and more. And six months later, I weighed in under the 200-pound mark for the first time in ten years.

My way too tolerant husband finally put his foot down and insisted that I come to my senses and make food for the family. My children were using any excuse to visit friends and eat "real" food. They were happy for my success but it wasn't working for our family. I knew he was right. The Monster had to go!

So I started adding cooked meals back in the evenings. It was hard. I have an addictive personality and it was not fun to set cooked "poison" on my table every night. But we still had smoothies in the morning and healthy lunches. After thirty days, my children were glowing and happy and bringing their friends to our house again. My husband was happy and none of us were dead or diagnosed with some awful cooked food disease.

I maintained my 100% raw through my next two pregnancies and was mainly raw for my last sweet Pure Market Express baby in 2010. Now, I eat pretty much as I wish but my tastes run predominantly raw. I love smoothies and salads and raw sweets of course. To date, my weight loss stands at about 165 pounds. I'm not 100% raw but I feel incredible and I try to let my body dictate what I eat.

I remember the first time a raw teacher told me to go to the grocery store and listen to what my body wanted. My body clearly, very distinctly said, "Doritos and cookie dough please." Hmmmm. But the longer I was raw, the more I found that to be true.

One summer, I practically subsisted on cherries and grapes. When I was pregnant with baby #7, I ate three to four avocados a day and still managed to deliver a sweet 7.7 lb boy and was 15 pounds lighter on the day I gave birth than the day I got pregnant. Sometimes, salads rule my world and other times it's all raw cookies all the time. We have fun with food now. We play with it and create new and interesting recipes – some raw and some not. Balance is the word. Balance wins the day.

In today's world of highly processed, chemical laden, genetically modified Franken "food", I truly believe it is more important to KNOW where your food comes from and, if possible, help produce it than being 100% raw ever was. If I wouldn't put a single ingredient on my plate by itself, I try not to eat it. When is the last time you ordered a side of ferrous sulfite or succinic acid with your meal? Slathered your bread with it?

My basic rule of thumb is if I can't pronounce it, I probably shouldn't ingest it. If Americans could just accomplish that, the SAD (Standard American) diet would be a thing of the past. Pure Market Express was born of a desire to help people do just that. We wanted to show people just how easy and yummy healthy eating could be; to inspire people to play with their food! Our mission was to change the face of health in America. For four years, we loved, created and prepared goodies for thousands of people across the country.

I know healthy living can taste just as good and be just as crave-worthy as any box or drive-through. I know it doesn't have to be time consuming or difficult. My soul hurts to see the state of the health of our nation and see people turning to pills, stomach stapling and useless fads and gadgets to fix it.

Eventually, Quentin and I had to ask the very hard but very necessary question: are we really having an impact on the problem? For the families that ordered regularly, I knew that made a huge difference for them and I lived under the starfish philosophy for a long, long time. You know the old story about the child throwing a starfish back into the ocean and the old man asking him why he was doing it since it wasn't going to make any difference. The child just smiled and said, "it made a difference to that one" as he threw another starfish back into the water.

But I also knew from experience with "programs" myself that if I was dependent on them and for any reason they were not available, that my addictive self saw that as permission to go back to my old icky ways of eating. Okay, so how could Pure Market Express kitchen change things? I believe we need to empower those we are blessed to connect with.

I am a huge proponent of empowerment. We homeschool our seven children because we want them to learn to THINK; not to depend on rote knowledge or regurgitated facts but instead upon their ingenuity, creativity and ability to FIND the answer they need and if no answer exist's to CREATE the answer they need.

One of the most depressing, irritating statements I hear is "I can't", but even worse, like nails on the chalkboard of my mind is "I can't because _____". I can't because I don't like health food. I can't because my kids won't like it. I can't because I am too busy. I can't because I don't know how.

For those of you who know me personally and have seen someone say one of those things to me, you may have witnessed my eyes glaze momentarily while my brain screams YES YOU CAN! Then I put my arm around their shoulder and show them all the yummy goodies we could create to open their eyes and their taste buds to the world of radiant living.

Nine times out of ten, the person would walk away knowing that I, Rebecca, can create yummy healthy food. They would leave just as convinced that I was different and THEY could never do such a thing. They weren't talented enough or didn't know enough or any one of a zillion excuses not to make a change. It was always that special 10th person whose eyes would light up with amazement and empowerment that would fill my heart and keep me going.

Self-empowerment is woven into my soul. I can do anything, learn anything, accomplish anything I set my mind to. And so can anyone else. Regardless of my past, my less than perfect growing up, limited opportunities, being fat, losing a child, blah blah blah. Hard? Yes. An excuse for not trying?
Absolutely not. I CAN OVERCOME AND SO CAN YOU. This is the mantra of my soul.

"I can't because..." makes me want to do backflips of frustration. I don't need anyone to take care of me. I need support, guidance, love, coaching but a hand out? Never. Don't GIVE me the answer - show me how to FIND the answer. That is love. It is not easy but it is love.

They say if you give a man a fish, you feed him for a day; teach a man to fish, you feed him for a lifetime. Pure Market Express spent four years selling the proverbial fish.

That will not change the world. We were only one in a huge marketplace of people hawking their own fish. I passionately truly believe that anyone can learn to easily incorporate healthy radiant eating habits into their life and thereby revolutionize their health. I cannot give up the mission but the time has come to change the method. I can teach people to find/create/manifest their OWN proverbial fish. This book is the beginning of that new mission.

The recipes that follow are exactly the recipes we used in the Pure Market Express kitchen. They are designed to be made quickly and easily. Most recipes are pretty self-explanatory but if they are especially difficult (i.e., Cinnamon Rolls or Pecan Pie) I noted that in the recipe.

These are recipes that I have loved for years, some are my personal creation, some were born of the inspiration of another cookbook, blog or chef and some are the complete and total creation of those wonderful souls who have come through our kitchen in the last four years. I have played with them endlessly and what you read here is the way I would make them for myself.

However, I believe recipes are like clothes. We all wear clothes and the basic components are the same: underwear, something on the bottom and something on the top. There may even be similarities or obvious inspiration in our outfits but we all wear things differently. We play and change and create a look totally our own. Our personality and individuality comes through in the way we choose to wear something that is totally unique.

So it is with recipes. There are 100 recipes for lasagna in 100s of cookbooks and they are all 98% identical but each chef has put their individual stamp on each one. So it is with raw food, PLAY with these recipes and make them your own! Nothing would please my heart more than if you were inspired by a recipe in this book but tweaked in just the right way to make it yours and serve it to your friends.

And when they love it (and they will) and they ask (which they will), "whose recipe is this?" Say, "It's my creation – isn't it yummy?" Because it is! If I or the recipes in this book can provide the inspiration for your creation, then I am blessed and my mission is accomplished.

The three steps to radiant eating are:

1. Get inspired.

2. Play with your food – make it divinely YOU!

3. Kill the Food Monster! Focus on the good, the positive, the fabulous choices you are making and let the rest go. One bad food decision isn't the end of the world. It won't kill you and it is absolutely no reason to run to a drive-through window!

Words cannot express how blessed I am to be a part of your radiant journey. There is so much love wrapped into each of these recipes, I pray you are inspired to begin, begin again or keep dancing on your personal path to health!

Radiantly yours,

Rebecca

Rebecca

EQUIPMENT LIST

Bowls, cutting boards and good knives. These are a given for anyone in the kitchen but there are some big differences with the equipment you use for raw "cooking." This is a list of ideal equipment and sub ideas.

Machines:

1. HIGH-POWERED BLENDER: We started with Vitamix of course but I have found Blentec and Waring to be excellent models as well. If you have one solid blender, if necessary, you can do without a food processor and a Magic Bullet. Try to get a large carafe and a small carafe if you are going to do this to give you a bit more flexibility. (Note: We will use a blender and Vitamix interchangeably.)

2. FOOD PROCESSOR: We used Cuisinart but I think any kind would probably work. The key here is a BIG enough food processor. When I first started making raw dishes, I had a 2 cup food processor and I could NOT figure out how people were getting so much food through the darn thing. I had never actually used one before and didn't realize how big they came. You'll find 12-14 cup sizes ideal for cracker recipes but 4-6 cups is very functional as well. You'll just need to do smaller batches through it.

3. MAGIC BULLET/BELLA BLENDER/NINJA: Basically a smaller blender for herbs and garlic and ginger and such that will be hard to spin down in a Vitamix or food processor. Not necessary, just nice.

4. DEHYDRATOR – Excalibur or Cabela's brand

a. Your oven can do a perfectly fine job here with a bit of experimentation AND you might check things like Craigslist or Ebay just before and after the holiday as this tends to be something people will purchase and then not use as much as they would like and they try to get rid of it.

b. Note: My Cabela's brand dehydrator did NOT come with teflex sheets so I wrapped them in plastic wrap and it worked just fine and clean up was a breeze – yay!

5. JUICER – ideally a centrifugal like a Breville AND a twin gear like a Green Star.

a. If you have one or the other, the recipes will still work. I love having both if possible because the twin gear does wonderfully with hard veggies like carrots and beets but struggles with fruits. The centrifugal does a lovely job with fruits but I find with carrots especially the pulp is a bit wet for using in things like Pumpkin Pie or Sushi. No worries – just give the pulp a good wringing out in a nut milk bag to remove the extra juice and you'll be fine.

6. VEGETABLE SPIRALIZER – very handy for making pasta. I remember the first time I got a blister from making so much pasta for orders!

a. If you don't want to make this investment, you can use a potato slicer for a linguini noodle.

7. MANDOLIN: Now that I cook mostly from home I use a variable Sharper Image mandolin that I am pretty pleased with.

a. If you really don't want to purchase one of these, the alternative is to slice your veggies super thin. I personally don't have the knife skills to manage a thin enough cut but I know it is possible.

GADGETS:

1. SMALL ICE CREAM SCOOP – I bought mine from Pampered Chef. Fabulous tool! We used it constantly.

2. NUT MILK BAG – I always have two on hand just in case one develops a hole. I actually bought a bunch of tulle on sale at a fabric store to make nut milk bags from; a Super inexpensive solution and, best of all, I could make any size I wanted.

3. PERFECT BROWNIE – this is a brownie cutter I saw on an infomercial once and it is the bomb for scoring crackers. Maybe Santa could bring you one?

4. GLOVES – any kind latex or non-latex glove.

Breakfest

I am a smoothie girl. I adore a smoothie first thing in the morning. However, there are times when just a smoothie won't do. These breakfast recipes are challenging but the most awesome-est part about them is that each and every one can be prepared ahead of time and frozen or stored on the counter for just the right moment when you are wanting something decadent or more substantial to begin your day. They make a wonderful Saturday afternoon project but once they are done – you will be blessed for weeks. Try the recipe once, then play with it of course – then make it times four and you will be set up!

Banana Breakfast Crepes

Degree of Difficulty: Moderately difficult

Have these rollups waiting when you roll out of bed. Rich banana filling finds a bright complement in strawberry puree. Yummy hidden healthy ingredients while French crepes the not-so-hidden inspiration.

4 cups bananas, over ripe
3/4 cup agave nectar, divided
2 cups cashews, soaked
1+ cup water (as needed)
2 tablespoons lemon juice
1 tablespoon tamari
1/4 teaspoon vanilla beans
2 cups strawberries, frozen

Procedure

Set frozen strawberries aside in a bowl to soften.

For crepe shells

1. Place bananas in food processor and blend until smooth with 1/4 cup agave nectar.
2. Spread about 1/8 inch thick onto a teflex sheet on a dehydrator screen.
3. Dehydrate about 12 hours. Should be formed, pliable and solid - not crispy.
4. Remove and slice into squares approximately 3" by 3" to form crepes.

For the filling

1. In Vitamix, blend cashews, lemon, tamari, water, vanilla and 1/4 cup agave nectar until totally smooth.
2. Set filling aside in a separate bowl.
3. Blend strawberries and remaining 1/4 cup agave to make topping.

Assembly

1. On serving platter, spread a thin blended strawberry topping across the platter.
2. Lay one crepe flat, fill with 1-2 tablespoons of cashew filling and roll like a cigar.
3. Place the rolled crepe seam side down on the platter of strawberry.
4. Repeat to utilize all crepes and filling.
5. * Drizzle remaining topping on top of rolled crepes.
6. Gnosh.

Oven Temperature: 105°F

Recipe Tips

** When you make the crepe filling, process until very loose then pick up the dehydrator tray and tilt it to create an even crepe.
** This is a great one to make and freeze. When you are ready, let it thaw in the fridge over-night and top with fresh strawberries for breakfast! YUM!
** This recipe was inspired by the Strawberry Crepe in Alissa Cohen's first book. Ours omits the honey for a completely vegan dish and used cashews but Alissa's genius is all over the final creation. I was privileged to attend one of her five-day workshops early in my raw food journey. I am so grateful to inspiring pioneers like Alissa for forging the trail for me!

Reviews

These were absolutely yummy, another I will definitely purchase again. I was impressed how delicious they were. - E. Wald
Wonderful! These are SO good. I couldn't limit myself to one serving of two crepes, and ended up eating three! Definitely on my favorites list! - S. Robertson
Amazing breakfast or dessert! Loved the creamy filling and sauce. - JA Smith

Cherry Honey Crunch Bars

Degree of Difficulty: Moderately difficult

Move over granola bars - you got nothin' on our breakfast bar bliss!

2 cups chopped almonds
1 cup cashews, ground to flour
1/2 cup agave nectar
1/2 cup sesame seeds
1/2 cup cherries, dried
1/4 cup golden flaxseed, soaked
1 tablespoon maca
1/8 teaspoon vanilla beans
1/4 teaspoon sea salt

Frosting:
1/2 cup coconut butter
1/4 cup honey (or agave)
1/2 cup maple syrup

Procedure

1. Soak flax in 1 cup of warm water.
2. Pulse chopped almonds in the food processor into chunky pieces.
3. Process cashews in blender to flour. Be careful not to over process and make cashew butter.
4. Mix almonds, cashews, sesame seeds, flax, maca, agave, vanilla, sea salt.
5. Fold in chopped dried cherries.
6. Spread on teflex sheet approximately 1/2 inch thick - should be about the thickness of a granola bar.
7. Dehydrate 12 hours or overnight. Pull your trays out of the dehydrator for frosting.
8. Place frosting ingredients in food processor and process until smooth.
9. Frost bars in criss-crossing pattern about a quarter inch apart.
10. Place in dehydrator for another 12 hours to set the frosting.

11 Cut and store in refrigerator. Can also be frozen for future use.

Oven Temperature: 105°F

Recipe Tips

** When mixing dough, I like to use gloves and really get in there with my hands. However, a KitchenAid mixer with a dough hook works especially well too!
** The frosting should be relatively loose so you can drizzle with a spoon to make a criss-cross pattern. You could also use a frosting piping set or even totally frost the top - you decide!
** Should be stored flat to minimize frosting sticking the bars together.
** Can be frozen for future use.

Review

Delicious. So much flavor and honey gooeyness.
- J. Kerrine

Cinnamon Rolls

Degree of Difficulty: Moderately difficult

Sweet glory, there's nothing that can't be made raw! Almond meal, ground flaxseed and dates form buns atop which you can lay a sweet frosting canopy. The only thing missing from the experience is the guilt, and who needs that??

Dough
1 cup Brazil nuts
1 cup brown flaxseed, ground
2 tablespoons extra virgin olive oil
1 tablespoon coconut butter
1-1/2 teaspoons cinnamon
1/4 teaspoon sea salt
1/8 teaspoon cayenne (just a pinch!)

Filling
1 cup dates, soaked
1/4 cup water
1 tablespoon cinnamon
1/4 teaspoon vanilla bean
1/2 cup chopped walnuts
1/2 cup chopped raisins

Maple frosting
1 cup cashews, soaked
1/2 cup maple syrup
2 tablespoons coconut butter
2 tablespoons water
1/4 teaspoon vanilla beans
1/8 teaspoon cinnamon

Procedure
1. Grind flax in waring blender.
2. Add cayenne, salt and 1-1/2 teaspoons cinnamon.
3. Process Brazil nuts, olive oil and coconut butter until smooth and soupy.
4. HAND mix Brazil nut mixture with flaxseed mixture.
5. Process all filling ingredients until smooth.
6. While filling is processing chop walnut's and mix in a small bowl with raisins.
7. Mix approximately half of the filling into the dough mixture by hand.
8. Roll out dough into a 9x11 inch rectangle between two teflex sheets.
9. Spread remaining filling over the rolled out dough.
10. Sprinkle walnut/raisin mixture over filling.
11. Now slowly, using the teflex sheet like a sushi roller, roll the dough tightly like a cinnamon roll.
12. When you finish rolling, wrap tightly in plastic wrap and refrigerate overnight.
13. Cut into 1 inch rolls. Top with Maple Frosting and dig in!

Recipe Tips
** This recipe works best if you are willing to work the dough with your hands.
** Roll out the dough on a teflex sheet from your dehydrator. If you don't have teflex, spread some coconut oil on your cutting board to prevent the dough from sticking to the board.
** Dough will be moderately sticky. If your rolling pin is sticking directly on the dough, cover it with teflex and roll through the teflex. If you don't have teflex, use a large piece of plastic wrap.
** This is a great recipe to quadruple and freeze! Then you can have a cinnamon roll any time you please!

Reviews
Wonderful rolls ... magnificent sauce! The cinnamon rolls, on their own, are very tasty... but it's the sauce that arrives with them that helps this duo take the cake! Great texture and taste - Beth, Richardson, TX
These taste good. Very moist and sweet. - Carmen, Arlington,
It's like a raw vegan Hostess Coffee Cake! Remember those little coffee cakes - chewy and crumbly and oh-so-cinnamony all at the same time? These are exactly like that, except better! No oils or preservatives, just amazing good-for-you deliciousness. - Mission Viejo, CA

Cocogurt

Degree of Difficulty: Easy

Our raw plain yogurt makes a beautiful parfait layered with fresh fruit, enriches homemade smoothies or stands in for sour cream. Coconut meat, coconut water and lemon juice are blended until smoother than smooth.

2 cups slightly sour coconut meat
1/2 cup water
2 tablespoons lemon juice

Procedure
Blend until smooth.

Recipe Tips
** Use this instead of Greek yogurt in your smoothies.

Review
Rich and filling, tastes like you're eating a lot of calories. I eat it with bananas and cinnamon. I usually would eat 1/3 at a time. Very filling. - K. Rush, Stillwater, MN

Count Rawcula

Degree of Difficulty: Moderately difficult

Some mornings call for a simple bowl of cereal. This bowl begins with buckwheat, which gets marinated in raw chocolate. Pour on fresh nut milk (your own), add some berries or sliced banana if you like, and spoon up a smile.

4 cups buckwheat
1/2 cup cacao
1/2 cup honey or agave nectar
3/4 teaspoon vanilla beans
1/2 teaspoon sea salt

Procedure
1. Measure buckwheat into a glass bowl. Cover with warm water several inches over the buckwheat.
2. Soak for at least 4 hours up to 24 hours.
3. Drain and rinse thoroughly.
4. * Be careful if you allow the buckwheat to sprout that you only allow a teeny tiny little tail - anything more will make it bitter.
5. Marinate the sprouted buckwheat in remaining ingredients for at least 4 more hours.
6. Spread on dehydrator teflex sheets in granola- type chunks. Mixture will be VERY juicy. Spread carefully.
7. Dehydrate at 105°F degrees until crispy, approximately 24 hours.

Recipe Tips
** This will smell AMAZING. Try not to eat it all straight out of the dehydrator.
** Remember you can use an oven at the lowest setting with a slightly open door if you don't have a dehydrator.

Review
Confession: I love this cereal so much that I thought I could learn to replicate it myself. Impossible. Just do yourself a favor and buy a family size (-or two like me...). If it becomes comfort food for you too, then you'll slice bananas on top and float it in unsweetened vanilla almond milk. You will be happy, you will be happy, you will be happy, you will find a spoon. - Rochelle C., New York, NY

Donut Holes

Degree of Difficulty: Moderately difficult

Among our customers' craves and faves, our doughnut holes so closely resemble the real ones, you'll be basking in bakery bliss. Nut pulp does dough duty, while a pass through the dehydrator provides outer crisp. "Coffee" break, anyone?

5 cups Brazil nuts
1/2 cup maple syrup
1/2 cup coconut oil, melted
1/4 teaspoon sea salt

Topping
1 tablespoon sucanat
1 tablespoon cinnamon
1/4 teaspoon nutmeg

Procedure

1. Process Brazil nuts in food processor until finely ground.
2. Add maple syrup, coconut oil and salt and process again.
3. Use an ice cream scoop to scoop dough out of the bowl.
4. Roll it until it makes a tight, even donut hole shape.
5. * This works best if you wear plastic gloves.
6. * You may need to squeeze a bit of liquid out of the dough if was over-processed and the Brazil nuts have released oil.
7. Dehydrate 24 hours.
8. Mix cinnamon, sucanat and nutmeg in a Magic Bullet or with a mortar and pestle until powdery.
9. Now gently roll dehydrated donut holes through the topping being careful not to break the donut holes.
10. Dehydrate for another 24 hours.

Oven Temperature: 105°F

Recipe Tips

If you don't have a small ice cream scoop, (I love the one from Pampered Chef), you can use a small melon baller or a tablespoon.

Review

They are that good. Seriously. I have attempted to bake gluten-free, vegan donut holes and donuts over the past several years and none of them have even come close to tasting as good as these do. I first bought these at a local store and after tasting them I decided that I needed to start ordering regularly from Pure Market Express and try out all of their wonderful items. - Moorhead, MN

Delightful cinnamon breakfast/dessert. I can't believe how much they taste like real doughnut holes right down to the texture. Addictive!
- AM Day, Baraboo,

French Toast Oatmeal

Degree of Difficulty: Easy

Retire your fork and call into service your spoon. We doctor and dress up a bowl of oatmeal with raisins, cinnamon, maple syrup and vanilla, inviting you to add berries or whipped cream as the last word.

4 cups rolled oats
1 cup raisins
1/2 cup maple syrup
1 tablespoon cinnamon
1/8 teaspoon vanilla beans

Procedure

1. Place all ingredients in a large bowl and hand toss until well combined.
2. Store in freezer bags in the freezer or in an air tight container in the refrigerator.

Recipe Tips

** Soak in your favorite nut milk to soften. Can warm in a saucepan or in the dehydrator if desired.
** I love mine with fresh fruit!

Maple Apple Crepes

Degree of Difficulty: Moderately difficult

No better way to start the day than guilt-free maple frosting drenched goodness! Fruity. Spicy. Creamy. The adjectives spill sweetly from these breakfast rollups that taste fresh out of the crepe pan. Apple and maple are longtime friends, and their pairing here lifts the experience even higher.

Crepe
3 cups Young Thai coconut meat
1 cup red apples
1 cup water
1 cup golden flaxseed, measure then grind
2 teaspoons cinnamon

Filling
2 cups red apples, skin on
1/2 cup walnuts
1/4 cup raisins
1 tablespoon maple syrup
1 tablespoon lemon juice
1/4 teaspoon lemon zest
1/4 teaspoon cinnamon

Frosting
1 cup soaked cashews
1/2 cup maple syrup
2 tablespoons coconut butter
2 tablespoons water
1/4 teaspoon vanilla beans
1/8 teaspoon cinnamon

For the Crepes

1. Blend coconut meat, apple and enough water to make it smooth.
2. Transfer to mixing bowl and fold in remaining ingredients.
3. Spread approximately 3 cups thinly on teflex and dehydrate for at least 12 hours, until firm but still flexible.

For the Fillng

Shred apples with your food processor shredding attachment. Toss with remaining filling ingredients.

For the Frosting

1. Blend all frosting ingredients till smooth.
2. Try not to hurt yourself as you clean out the carafe with your fingers just like when you were a kid.

Oven Temperature: 105°F

Pancakes

Degree of Difficulty: Moderately difficult

A short stack it's not, but our hotcakes nonetheless deliver fresh-off-the-griddle flavor studded with bursts of chocolate or blueberry heaven.

2 medium bananas
2 cups pecans
2 cups macadamia nuts, can substitute cashews
1 cup dried blueberries, can use fresh or frozen
1 cup water
1/2 cup agave nectar
1/2 of a vanilla bean
3/4 teaspoon sea salt

Procedure

1. In the Vitamix, process all ingredients EXCEPT blueberries until completely smooth. This will take multiple batches through the Vitamix.
2. ** May need to fill the Vitamix carafe more than once.
3. In the food processor, process blueberries until they are small and chunky.
4. ** If using frozen or fresh, GENTLY fold into your batter. Mixing too vigorously will turn your pancakes purple.
5. Fold into pancake batter.
6. On a teflex sheet, spread 1/4 cup batter in a pancake shape and smooth edges with a wet spoon.
7. After 24 hours, gently flip the pancakes and dehydrate the other side for another 24 hours. Finished pancakes will be soft and flexible but not wet or mushy.

Recipe Tips

** If you start these on Friday night and flip on Saturday, you could enjoy WARM yummy raw pancakes for Sunday brunch!
** Try mixing flavors, use chocolate chips instead of blueberries or dried strawberries even - YUM!

Reviews

Would give more stars if possible! Yum! - Emily B., St. Paul, MN
These cakes satisfy that need for something comforting to start the day. A homage to traditional hotcakes, this maple goodness is balanced with tart blueberries. A little goes a long way...
- Rochelle C., New York, NY

These are really amazing. They have a lot of taste and really do taste like pancakes. They are quite sweet so maybe they honey isn't necessary.
- Denise, New Providence, NJ

Strawberry Crunch

Degree of Difficulty: Moderately difficult

No artificial flavors here! A whole cup of fresh strawberries tart up the sweet syrup in which buckwheat clusters marinate before being dehydrated to a crisp. Douse with your own fresh nut milk and spoon up a smile.

5 cups buckwheat
4 cups strawberries
1 cup honey or agave nectar
1 teaspoon vanilla beans
1/2 teaspoon sea salt

Procedure

1. Measure buckwheat into a glass bowl. Cover with warm water several inches over the buckwheat.
2. Soak for at least 4 hours up to 24 hours.
3. Drain and rinse thoroughly.
4. * Be careful if you allow the buckwheat to sprout that you only allow a teeny tiny little tail - anything more will make it bitter.
5. Blend 2 cups of the strawberries to create a puree.
6. Then marinate the soaked buckwheat in strawberry puree, vanilla, sea salt and sweetener of choice for at least 4 more hours.
7. Muddle remaining 2 cups strawberries and fold into the marinade mixture.
8. Spread on dehydrator teflex sheets in granola type chunks. Mixture will be VERY juicy. Spread carefully.
9. Dehydrate at 105 degrees until crispy.

Oven Temperature: 105°F

Recipe Tips

** This will smell AMAZING - like the best strawberry candle ever. Try not to eat it all straight out of the dehydrator.

** Remember you can use an oven at the lowest setting with a slightly open door if you don't have a dehydrator.

Review

Confession: I love this cereal so much that I thought I could learn to replicate it myself. Impossible. Just do yourself a favor and buy a family size (-or two like me...). If it becomes comfort food for you too, then you'll slice bananas on top and float it in unsweetened vanilla almond milk. You will be happy, you will be happy, you will be happy, you will find a spoon. - Rochelle C., New York, NY

Tennessee Grawnola

Degree of Difficulty: Moderately difficult

It's all here: pecans, raisins, dried apricots, sprouted buckwheat, raw honey and seeds galore (flax, sesame, pumpkin, sunflower). Swell alone. Satisfying with nut milk. And sweet crunch for ice cream sundaes or yogurt parfaits.

3-1/2 cups buckwheat, measure then sprout
1 cup raisins
1 cup chopped apricots, dried
1/2 cup extra virgin olive oil
1/2 cup honey
1/2 cup sesame seeds, measure then grind
1/2 cup chopped pumpkin seeds
1/2 cup chopped sunflower seeds
1/2 cup pecans
1 tablespoon vanilla beans
1/4 cup brown flax, measure then grind
2 teaspoons cinnamon

Procedure
1. Measure buckwheat. Cover with warm water several inches higher than the buckwheat in the bowl. Soak for 24 hours.
2. Drain and rinse thoroughly. Set aside in a large glass bowl.
3. Chop nuts and dried fruits and add to buckwheat.
4. Grind brown flaxseed in the Vitamix and add to buckwheat mixture.
5. Add honey, olive oil, cinnamon and sea salt to buckwheat mixture.
6. Mix thoroughly with gloved hands, making sure to incorporate all ingredients.
(** could also use a KitchenAid mixer with the dough hook.)
7. Spread on teflex sheets in granola-type chunks.
8. Dehydrate at 105 degrees for 12 hours. Flip your trays and dehydrate for another 12 hours to make sure both sides are done.
9. Can be stored on the counter in an airtight container or in the freezer for longer life.
10. Serve with nut milk or as a snack on the go.

Oven Temperature: 105°F

garlic crackers
corn chips
Crackers Chips & Cereal
pizza chips

Snacks and Crackers!

They are must have for life right? Whether it is to slather some cheese on or build your very own raw BLT – crackers must be present. And remember the last time you were out running around and found yourself reaching for the chips or the store-bought bread? Not anymore. These treats are great to keep in the car in your "E-bag"! An E-bag is that lovely container in every health conscious person's car or truck or backpack or purse with healthy goodies just in case timeframes get stretched and we find ourselves starving surrounded by gas stations and fast food.

All the dehydrated goodies are designed to go in a square dehydrator such as an Excalibur or a Cabela's on trays with teflex and mesh sheets.

If you do not have a dehydrator, never fear. Eggplant Bac'Un may still be in your future. Simply turn your oven on to the lowest possible heat and place your tray of goodies inside. Leave the door open a touch to encourage air flow. This is a much faster process so make sure you check on your goodies every hour until you get a feel for how long the dehydration will take in your oven.

Butter Walnut Bread

Degree of Difficulty: Easy

5 cups walnuts
2-1/2 cups butternut squash, peeled and cut into 1-inch cubes
2-1/2 cups zucchini
1 cup golden flaxseed
1/2 cup hemp seeds
1 cup water
1 teaspoon sea salt

Procedure

1. Soak walnuts for at least 1 hour in warm water, enough to cover.
2. Grind golden flaxseeds in Vitamix.
3. Process all ingredients in the food processor to make a chunky dough.
4. Dough should NOT be smooth. You should be able to still basically identify all the basic ingredients except the flaxseed & salt.
5. Spread 3/8 inch thick on teflex sheets, score and dehydrate at 105 for 12 hours, flip and dehydrate for another 12 hours.

Recipe Tips

This was one of the first recipes I made when I was searching for a raw "bread." While it is not squishy, stick to the roof of your mouth like Wonder Bread, you can make it as strong as you wish by increasing the thickness of the dough on your Teflex sheet. A thinner spread will make a delicate buttery cracker perfect for a cucumber sandwich or olive tapenade. A thicker spread will hold up to an entire sandwich - YUM!
** I prefer to score these before dehydrating. I think it speeds the process and also because the dough is chunky, it can get too crumbly to cut after it is totally dry.
** If you choose to pre-score, check out a Perfect Brownie cutter. I love that thing

Chili Lime Crackers

Degree of Difficulty: Moderately difficult

Great on their own or a perfect match for Pure Market Express Cilantro Jalapeño Cheese!

4 cups buckwheat, sprouted
2 cups zucchini, chopped
1 cup golden flaxseed, ground
1 cup tomatoes
1 cup cashews, soaked
1/2 cup pumpkin seeds
1/4 cup lime juice
1/4 cup extra virgin olive oil
2 tablespoons cumin
2 tablespoons honey
2 teaspoons sea salt
1 teaspoon chili powder
chili powder for sprinkling
1/2 teaspoon cayenne
2 cloves garlic

Procedure

1. Soak buckwheat in 8 cups warm water for 24 hours. Drain and rinse thoroughly.
2. Blend all ingredients in food processor, EXCEPT pumpkin seeds, in batches to create a chunky dough. This will take several batches through the food processor.
3. Place all processed ingredients in a large bowl.
4. Then rough chop pumpkin seeds in food processor and fold into other ingredients.
5. Spread on teflex sheets. Score into 3x3 crackers. Dehydrate until crispy - about 12 hours at 105 degrees.
6. Spray with lime juice and then sprinkle (very lightly) some chilli powder on top.
7. Dehydrate again until crispy - approximately another 12 hours.
8. Store in an airtight container on your container or in the freezer for anything over one month of storage.

Oven Temperature: 105°F

Recipe Tips

** This is the first recipe that I learned how important tasting your raw food recipe was at every step. With traditional cooking, flavors can change dramatically in the cooking or baking process but with raw food, you can get a pretty solid idea of what your dish will taste like from the dough. If the dough is good, the crackers will be good!

Corn Chips

Degree of Difficulty: Easy

5 cups corn, fresh off the cob or frozen
1 cup yellow onions, peeled and chopped
1/2 cup golden flaxseed, ground
1/4 cup lime juice
2 + 1 teaspoons sea salt
6 cloves garlic

Procedure

1. Grind flaxseed in Vitamix.
2. Process remaining ingredients in the food processor.

** Taste dough - should have a salty flavor - think Fritos.

3. Spread 2 cups thinly on Teflex sheets thinly, approximately 1/8 of an inch thick.
4. Score and dehydrate for 12 hours at 105 degrees.
5. Flip the chip and sprinkle with a light dusting of salt. Be CAREFUL! This is a thin chip; it is easy to over salt.
6. Dehydrate for another 6-12 hours until crispy.

Oven Temperature: 105°F

Recipe Tips

I love to experiment with this chip. I have added cilantro and/or jalapeños to make "green" corn chips or fold in some tomato for pretty red chunks. Let your imagination run!

Reviews

Just add salsa and you will feel like you're at a Mexican restaurant. Perfect for an after work/school snack. I finished mine before I had a chance to try it with guacamole so I'm buying some more. - Antioch, TN

I was so tempted to eat the entire box when they arrived today, but I just had to save some for my husband. I know he will be as impressed as I am with the light, crispy texture and wonderful taste. I've tried a lot of raw crackers that I didn't much care for but these are superb. You'd never even know they are healthy and raw. Not for those who don't enjoy snacks that are fairly salty. - Gentry, AZ

Perfect, crisp corn chip. Love the flavor and the crunch. Dip Happy! - AM Day, Baraboo, WI

Garlic Crackers

Degree of Difficulty: Moderately difficult

So often cast to the side—of our lasagna and ravioli, for instance—raw garlic bread is a wonder in its own right. Flavored just robustly enough, it's semi-chewy yet holds together when on sauce-mop-up duty.

6 cups zucchini
6 cups butternut squash, peeled and cut into 1-inch cubes
5 cups buckwheat, sprouted
1 cup yellow onions
1 cup water
1 cup golden flaxseed, ground
6-8 cloves garlic
3 tablespoons Italian seasoning
1 teaspoon sea salt
1 tablespoon garlic, powder

Procedure

1. Soak buckwheat in 10 cups of warm water for at least 4 hours and up to 24. Drain and rinse thoroughly.
2. Blend buckwheat and veggies in food processor in batches with enough water to mix well.
3. Grind flaxseed separately in a blender and add to mixture.
4. Spread dough approximately 1/8 inch thick and score.
5. Dehydrate for 6 hours at 105 degree and flip and dehydrate for another 6-12 hours or until crispy.

Oven Temperature: 105°F

Review

I can't stand flax crackers, mostly because of the slimy texture. But these aren't bad at all and are the perfect means of getting Good as Gouda into my mouth. - KL Grady, Virginia Beach, VA

Goji Trail Mix

Degree of Difficulty: Very Easy

Banish the snack attack with this yummy superfood packed snack!

4 cups cashews
2 cups pistachios
1 cup cherries, dried
1 cup goji berries
1 cup raisins
1/2 cup cacao nibs
2 teaspoons sea salt

Italian Flax

Degree of Difficulty: Easy

Pick a dip, any dip, and these crackers are the perfect transportation!

2 cups tomatoes
2 cups golden flax, divided
1 cup 6 oz soaked tomatoes, sun-dried
1 medium zucchini
1 red bell pepper
1 bunch parsley
1 jalapeño pepper, cored and chopped (leave the seeds in for extra spice; scrape them out for a milder version)
1 date, pitted
2 tablespoons tamari
1 tablespoon oregano, dried
2 teaspoons basil, dried
2 cloves garlic
2 teaspoons sea salt

Procedure

1. Soak 1-1/2 cups flax seeds in 3 cups warm water for at least 1 hour.
2. Process all ingredients except flax seeds in the food processor until smooth. Then fold in flax seeds.
3. Spread approximately 3 cups on teflex sheet thinly.
4. Dehydrate for 12 hours at 105 degrees, flip and dehydrate until crispy - approximately another 6 hours.

Oven Temperature: 105°F

Recipe Tips

** This recipe is not able to be pre-scored. You will need to wait until the chips are done to cut or break them into bite size pieces.

Review

It took some self-control not to eat the whole container. The best part is the light crisp texture. They have a small kick of spice and are salty. - Angela, NY

Onion Bread

Degree of Difficulty:
Moderately difficult

Soft and chewy, these slices have better "bread" texture than many dehydrated alternatives. Sandwiches the likes of BLTs take kindly to the gentle onion flavor.

7 medium yellow onions, sliced
2 cups ground sunflower seeds
1 cup extra virgin olive oil
3/4 cup ground flaxseed, brown
1 teaspoon sea salt

Procedure

1. Grind flaxseeds in Vitamix.
2. Process 6 onions, flaxseeds, sunflower seeds and olive oil in food processor.
3. Cut remaining onion in half and thinly slice the remaining onion at 1.5 mm.
4. Mix with batter and spread thinly on teflex sheets.
5. Dehydrate for 12 hours at 105 degrees. Flip and dehydrate for another 6-12 hours.

Servings: 8

Oven Temperature: 105°F

Recipe Tips

Not surprisingly, this recipe was inspired by Matt Amsden at Rawvolution. He is wicked smart and this, in my humble opinion, is really a raw classic thanks to Matt.

Review

I love this bread. . . although it's more like a cracker, thin and crispy on my end. Great flavor, but I'm not sure my boyfriend likes my onion breath! - S. Robertson, Cordova, TN 8/22/2011

This bread is so delicious. Perfect soft chew. Great sandwich maker! Makes wonderful BLT's or just BL's w/out the T. I can definitely overindulge. - AM Day, Baraboo, WI 10/10/2012

I am new to raw foods, so this was my first time trying a raw "bread." I have been wanting to try to make one, but had no idea what it should taste and look like. Well, this onion bread is an amazing example of how good raw foods can be. The ingredients are so simple, it just amazes me how much flavor is packed into this bread. The texture is really nice too. I was worried that it was going to be super dense and weigh me down like flax pancakes do...but these are nice and light with a slight crispness. My only complaint is that the pieces in my box were broken and smaller than what I had expected, so it would be difficult to make a sandwich with them. But, I don't care. It is so good, I will make do with them as they are!! - Moorhead, MN

Pepperoni Bites

Degree of Difficulty: Moderately difficult

Truly one of the greats! Our raw pepperoni bites blend zucchini, almonds, dates, peppers and more to form these bite sized pizza blasts.

2 cups zucchini, peeled
1/2 cup almonds, soaked
1/2 red bell pepper seeded & cut into 1/4-inch cubes
1 date
1 teaspoon black pepper
1 teaspoon mustard seed
1 teaspoon fennel seeds
1 teaspoon pepper flakes
1 teaspoon sea salt
1 teaspoon paprika
1/4 teaspoon garlic, powder
1/8 teaspoon liquid smoke

Procedure

1. In food processor, grind the almonds to just slightly larger than rice size. Remove to mixing bowl.
2. Process zucchini, red pepper, and date till smooth.
3. Mix with ground almonds till a thick falafel-like paste forms.
4. Fold in all remaining ingredients.
5. Drop a tablespoon of the batter on teflex with a small ice cream scoop and flatten slightly to form rounds about the size of a slice of pepperoni.
6. Dehydrate for 12 hours at 105 degrees until crispy.
7. Store on the counter in an air tight container.

Oven Temperature: 105°F

Reviews

With a crunchy texture and strong pepperoni/pizza flavors, I feel like I'm eating a slice of the bad stuff. I've tasted others versions of raw vegan pepperoni and Pure Market Express's version is the best I've tasted. I'm so happy to have found a new comfort food. - V. Tow, Placeville, CA

These are powerful little bites: good pepperoni flavor -- too strong to eat on their own but add a lovely flavor to salads or raw pizza - JA Smith, Marcellus, MI

Insanely good! I love these and my non-raw family loved these too! Pretty spicy, crunchy-chewy and smoky! These are awesome.
- S. Nelson, St. Paul, MN

Pizza Chips aka Tostada

Degree of Difficulty: Easy

15 roma tomatoes
1 cup brown flaxseed, ground
1/4 cup golden flaxseed, soaked
1/4 cup extra virgin olive oil
1/4 cup pumpkin seeds
2 tablespoons tamari
1 tablespoon oregano, dried
1 tablespoon basil, dried
1 teaspoon black pepper
1/2 teaspoon sea salt

Procedure
1. Grind brown flaxseed in the blender. Set aside in a large glass bowl.
2. Pulse chop pumpkins seeds in the food processor to break them up.
3. Process all other ingredients in the food processor and mix thoroughly with ground flax and pumpkin seeds.
4. Spread thinly and dehydrate at 105 degrees for 6 hours. Flip and dehydrate till crispy.

Oven Temperature: 105°F

Recipe Tips
* If making tostada shells, spread into shells the size of a personal pan pizza on your teflex sheets.

Spicy Pepitas

Degree of Difficulty: Easy

Perfect on-the-go-snack to satisfy your craving!

4 cups pumpkin seeds, soaked
1 cup cilantro, minced
1 tablespoon chili powder
1 tablespoon garlic powder
1 teaspoon sea salt
2 teaspoons lime juice
1 teaspoon cayenne, to taste

Procedure
1. Soak pumpkin seeds for at least 2 hours, rinse, drain and place in a mixing bowl.
2. Combine all ingredients, toss well.
3. Let sit at room temp for 1 hour then toss again.
4. Dehydrate until completely crispy, approximately 12 hours at 105 degrees.

Oven Temperature: 105°F

Mariachi beat wrap
Creamy garlic dill pasta
Entrees
Pad Thai

Bac`Un Burgers

Degree of Difficulty: Moderately difficult

Mc-Who? This is a happy meal like no other! Served up with a bun, ketchup, and mustard of course!

Burger
2 cups carrot pulp
2 cups tomatoes, diced
2 cups sunflower seeds, ground to flour
2 cups cashews, ground to flour
1/2 cup Bac`Un, minced
1 cup red onions, minced
1 red bell pepper, diced
3 stalk celery, diced
4 cloves garlic
1 jalapeño pepper, deseeded
1/4 cup Cashew Butter

Burger Spice Mix
1 tablespoon apple cider vinegar
1 tablespoon tamari
1/2 teaspoon mustard seed
1/2 teaspoon coriander
1/2 teaspoon fennel seeds
1/2 teaspoon Hickory salt
1/3 teaspoon cumin

Bac'Un
1 eggplant, peeled and cut into 1.5 mm slices
1/4 cup ume plum vinegar
1/4 cup extra virgin olive oil
1/8 teaspoon cayenne

Make the Bac'Un
1. Peel the eggplant. Slice with a mandolin at 1.5 mm.
2. Marinate eggplant slices with ume plum vinegar, extra virgin olive oil and cayenne for at least 1 hour.
3. Lay slices flat on teflex and dehydrate at 105 degrees for 12 hours or until crispy.
4. Rough chop 1 cup of Bac'Un. Remaining Bac'Un can be stored on the countertop in an airtight container.

Make the Burger
1. Juice carrots, ideally with a twin gear juicer. Drink juice and reserve 2 cups pulp.
2. Grind sunflower seeds and cashews to flour in your blender.
3. Process remaining burger ingredients in the food processor. Place in a large glass bowl and set aside.
4. Make spice mix.
5. Fold spice mix and chopped Bac'Un into veggie cashew mixture.
6. With gloved hands, form "patties" and place in teflex sheets.
7. Dehydrate 12 hours at 105 degrees, flip and dehydrate approximately another 12 hours. Burgers should be crispy on the outside but not dried all the way through.
8. * Dehydrating too long will give you crackers - be careful!

Oven Temperature: 105°F

Recipe Tips
** Because these burgers are not completely dehydrated, they will go bad unlike most dehydrated goodies. Store extras in the freezer.

Bac`Un Jalapeño Poppers

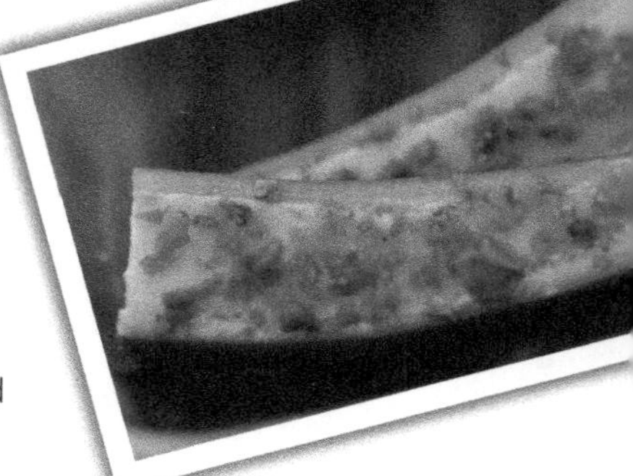

Degree of Difficulty: Easy

The leading appetizer on the Pure Market Express "Man Line" - we developed these to go with a good brew and a ball game. Seeded and deveined chunks of fresh jalapeño peppers filled with creamy nut cheese and topped with egg-plant bac'un - the perfect lunch for the quarterback on the field or in the armchair!

6-12 jalapeño peppers, deseeded and quartered

Bac'Un:
1 eggplant, peeled and cut into 1.5 mm slices
1/4 cup ume plum vinegar
1/4 cup extra virgin olive oil
1/8 teaspoon cayenne pepper

Filling:
2 cups cashews, soaked
1/4 cup red onions, minced
1/4 cup water, as needed
2 tablespoons nutritional yeast
2 tablespoons lemon juice
1 teaspoon salt

Procedure

Make the Bac'Un

1. Peel the eggplant. Slice with a mandolin at 1.5 mm.
2. Marinate eggplant slices with ume plum vinegar, extra virgin olive oil and cayenne for at least 1 hour.
3. Lay slices flat on teflex and dehydrate at 105 degrees for 12 hours or until crispy.
4. Rough chop 1 cup of Bac'Un. Remaining Bac'Un can be stored on the countertop in an airtight container.

Make the Jalapeño Cheese

1. Place cashews, water, lemon juice, nutritional yeast and salt in food processor.
2. Process till smooth adding water as needed.
3. Remove cheese to a bowl and fold in the diced red onion, 1/4 cup crumbled eggplant bac'un, and 1/2 jalapeño minced.
4. Set aside and prepare jalapeño peppers.

Stuff the Poppers

1. Put on gloves and slice jalapeños in half lengthwise, then cut them in half again across the width of the pepper so you have four poppers per pepper, each about 1.25 inches long.
2. Remove seeds and pith and rinse under cool water. Shake dry.
3. Fill each popper with approximately 1-1/2 teaspoons of popper cheese, filling pepper and making a small mound on top. Use a spoon or gloved hands to completely fill each popper and smooth the cheese.
4. Sprinkle minced Bac'Un on top.

Review

My husband & I are very new to the raw vegan lifestyle. He was quite skeptical of Pure Market's food. When he "tried" these poppers, he ate all of them & said he felt like he had just cheated. - E. Pullis, Bloomington, MN

These are super tasty, creamy, crunchy, and with the Bac'Un, just a bit smoky. They're wonderful, and eating the whole serving will definitely get your mouth warm! So close to the "real thing," yet more filling and energizing. - KL Grady, Virginia Beach, VA

Let me just say I am not a fan of jalapeños to begin with, but I tried it based on the reviews and let me tell you - I am on LOVE with this. Perfect texture, perfect size, and just enough spiciness that requires a glass of cold water. Do not pass this up! "Bac'Un" is super yummy! - Sarah T., Minneapolis, MN

Baked Mac-n-Cheese Pasta

Degree of Difficulty: Easy

The Cheeze:
1 cup cashews, soaked
1/2 cup water, as needed
1/2 red bell pepper
1/4 cup onions
1 tablespoon nutritional yeast
1tablespoon extra virgin olive oil
1 tablespoon tamari
1 teaspoon lemon juice
1/2 teaspoon turmeric
2 cloves garlic

The Pasta:
3 cups spiralized zucchini
3 tablespoons walnuts, chopped
1/2 teaspoon paprika

Make the Cheeze
Blend all ingredients till smooth.

Make the Pasta
1. Spiralize zucchini and rough chop to eliminate 8 foot noodles.
2. Sprinkle a pinch of paprika and 2 tablespoons chopped walnuts on top of zucchini.

Oven Temperature: 105°F

Review
Maybe doesn't taste exactly like macaroni and cheese, but delicious nonetheless. Very fresh tasting. I would definitely order it again. - Brigitt O., Minneapolis, MN
My kids devoured it (3 and 18 months) so you sure can't argue with that! - Gentry, AR
Whether or not this tastes like mac-n-cheese will depend on how long it has been since you had mac-n-cheese. It is a delightful and pleasing dish that underwhelms but is good for kids. - JA Smith, Marcellus, MI

Basil Fried Rice Recipe

Degree of Difficulty: Moderately difficult

The Rice:
3 cups parsnips, peeled
1 cup cashews
2 tablespoons lemon juice
1/2 teaspoon sea salt
The Toppings:
1 cup roma tomatoes
1 cup broccoli
1 cup portobello mushrooms
1/4 cup red onions
1/4 cup basil, chiffonade
1/4 cup cilantro

The Marinade:
1/2 cup lemon juice
1/4 cup tamari
1/4 cup agave nectar
1/4 cup sun-dried tomatoes
1 inch ginger root
1 teaspoon sea salt

The Sauce
1/8 cup basil, fresh
1/2 jalapeño chiles, stemmed, seeded and finely diced
1 tablespoon lemon juice
1 teaspoon cilantro
1/2 teaspoon red pepper flakes
1/2 teaspoon curry powder
1/4 teaspoon turmeric
1/4 teaspoon black pepper
1 clove garlic

Procedure:

The Rice

1. Chop parsnips in the food processor to a rice-like texture.
2. Add cashews and process again.
3. Toss with lemon juice and sea salt.
4. Set aside in a glass bowl.

Make the Marinade

1. Combine all marinade ingredients and blend.
2. Marinate portobello mushrooms and all toppings.

The Sauce:

1. Drain sun-dried tomatoes, reserve soak water.
2. Combine all sauce ingredients in blender. Blend till smooth.

Assemble

1. Remove veggies from marinade. Marinade may be stored for another batch for up to 30 days.
2. Toss rice with marinated veggies.
3. Fold in sauce.
4. Devour.

Recipe Tips

** The spice comes from the sauce in this dish. If you are unsure about spiciness, go easy on the sauce and add to desired heat level.

Review

Very tasty! Can't wait for my next order! This time I am ordering family size!!! - Porter Ranch, CA

This is so good! I was skeptical about fake rice :-) but this is so spicy and delicious with many complementing flavors. I'm not a fan of mushrooms but I was able to eat them in this entree with no problem. This settles my craving for spicy Thai food like Pad Kee Mao (drunken noodles)! - S. Nelson, St. Paul, MN

Big Greek Salad

Degree of Difficulty: Easy

A crunchy lunch from the heart of Greece! Just add your own fresh greens! Comes with enough dressing and toppings to make a family sized salad.

The Salad:
4 cups chopped romaine lettuce
1/2 cup tomatoes, diced
1/4 cup red onions, diced
2 tablespoons kalamata olives, pitted and sliced
1 teaspoon lemon juice
1 teaspoon extra virgin olive oil

The Dressing:
1/2 cup Cheese Base
1/4 cup water
1/4 cup red onions, minced
1-1/2 teaspoons Italian seasoning
1 clove garlic, minced
1/8 teaspoon sea salt

Procedure
1. Dice onion, tomatoes and olives.
2. Mix olive oil and lemon juice. Toss with onion/tomato mixture. Marinate while you make dressing.
3. Combine all dressing ingredients and blend until smooth. Set aside.
4. Chop romaine and toss with desired amount of dressing.
5. Top with tomato, olive and onion. YUM!

Oven Temperature: 105°F

Broccoli Salad

Degree of Difficulty: Easy

Perfect lunch after a workout or anytime!

The Salad:
2 cups broccoli, chopped
1/2 cup sunflower seeds
1/2 cup yellow onions
1/4 cup raisins

The Dressing:
1/2 cup cashews
2 tablespoons agave nectar
1 tablespoon apple cider vinegar
1/4 teaspoon sea salt
1/4 cup water as needed

Procedure
1. Chop broccoli, onion, and sunflower seeds roughly in food processor
2. Fold raisins in to chopped ingredients.
3. Blend the dressing ingredients until smooth.
4. Toss veggies with dressing and dig in.

Oven Temperature: 105°F

Caesar Salad

Degree of Difficulty: Easy

Toss yourself a classic. Our Caesar salad features a creamy dressing laced liberally with garlic. If it's possible for noontime eating to be both rich and light–and with raw "cooking," it most assuredly is–this is the poster dish.

The Salad:
4 cups romaine lettuce, chopped
1/2 cup tomatoes, diced
1/4 cup green olives, minced
2 tablespoons Bac`Un
2 tablespoons Zucchini Sprinkles

Give Unto Caesar Dressing:
1 cup cashews (pine nuts ROCK here if you are feeling decadent!)
1/3 cup extra virgin olive oil
1/3 cup water
2 tablespoons tamari
1 tablespoon flaxseed oil
2-1/2 tablespoons lemon juice
1/2 teaspoon sea salt
1/2 teaspoon black pepper
1 date
2-3 cloves garlic

Procedure
1. Chop 4 cups romaine lettuce
2. Blend all dressing ingredients until smooth and toss lettuce.
3. Dice tomatoes and olives.
4. Top dressed lettuce with diced lettuce and olives.
5. Sprinkle Bac'Un & Zucchini Sprinkles on top and dig in!

Recipe Tips
Zucchini Sprinkles are leftover peelings from organic zucchini tossed lightly with olive oil and Italian seasoning and dehydrated till crispy. USE everything

Chipotle Corn

Degree of Difficulty: Easy

3 cups corn, fresh off the cob or frozen
1 red bell pepper, diced
1 jalapeño pepper, seeded and diced
1/2 chipotle pepper, soaked and minced
2 tablespoons extra virgin olive oil
1 teaspoon black pepper
1/2 teaspoon sea salt

Procedure
1. Soak chipotle pepper.
2. Dice red bell pepper and jalapeños.
3. Mince soaked chipotle pepper
4. Toss all ingredients together.
5. Add salt and pepper to taste.

Oven Temperature: 105°F

Creamy Garlic Dill Pasta

Degree of Difficulty: Easy

3 cups zucchini, spiralized
1/4 cup avocados, cubed
1/4 cup tomatoes, diced
1 teaspoon dill

The Sauce:
1 cup cashews
1/2 cup onions
1/4 cup water
1 tablespoon lemon juice
1 tablespoon nutritional yeast
1 tablespoon dill, dried
1/2 teaspoon black pepper
1/4 teaspoon sea salt
3 cloves garlic

Procedure:
1. Spiralized zucchini.
2. Blend all sauce ingredients EXCEPT dill.
3. Fold dill into sauce.
4. Toss zucchini with sauce
5. Top with avocado, tomato and dill.
6. Dive in! Forks are optional.

Garlic Alfredo Pasta

Degree of Difficulty: Easy

Parmesan, butter, semolina fettuccine: Who needs it? A fresher concept for leaner, live-longer times, our version will leave you wanting for nothing except a napkin. Zucchini pasta twirls just like the real thing.

The Pasta:
3 cups spiralized zucchini
The Sauce:
1 cup water
1 cup cashews
1/4 cup onions
1/4 cup extra virgin olive oil
2 tablespoons lemon juice
2 teaspoons nutritional yeast
1/2 teaspoon black pepper
1/4 teaspoon sea salt
4-6 cloves garlic

Procedure
1. Spiralize approximately 2 zucchini.
2. Blend all sauce ingredients until smooth.
3. Toss with zucchini pasta.
4. Top with a sprinkle of Bac'Un - this will take the whole dish to a completely new level of YUM!

Fiesta Tostadas

Degree of Difficulty: Easy

A classic must have. If this is raw vegan, we can sign the world up!

1/2 cup Spicy Lentil Taco Meat
1/2 cup Lasagna Cheese
1 cup Sassy Salsa
3 tostada shells
toppings of your choice

Procedure

Assembly

1. One tostada shell, layer cheese, taco meat and salsa.
2. Add any other fresh veggies that please your palate such as jalapeños, sour cream, lettuce, or banana peppers.

Recipe Tips

** Okay, normally I seriously dislike having to go to other places in a recipe book for sub-recipes so I apologize in advance. However, the components prevented putting them all on one page. All I can say is that the minor inconvenience is SO worth it for the yummy meal that awaits you!
** The tostada shells will keep up to 90 days on the counter and the lasagna cheese and taco meat make relatively big batches that can be frozen for future use. The cool thing is now you have quick and easy raw awesomeness at your fingertips any time! Yay!

Review

This one won me over. I had it for breakfast. I am most picky first thing in the am. I wasn't sure what to think of the different packets of sauce and cheese and the topping. I assembled them onto 1 of the 3 tostada rounds and took a bite. MMMMM! I enjoyed the whole thing. Licked out the container and wished I had more. It was so creamy and flavorful. Even the tostada round itself was delicious alone. I liked the cilantro in the salsa and the peppery topping. Bring on some more!!! - J. Greene, Winter Haven, FL
Tastes like a day in the sunshine feels! These are really great. The cilantro laced salsa is crunchy and delicious, the "cheese" is really mild and actually tastes like cheese, and the "meat" is spiced heavily. These have a nice bite. - Denise, New Providence, NJ

I loved this so much! It's my favorite! Tastes and smells like the real thing! My husband was even shocked and he isn't a raw foodist!
- S. Jenkins, Titusville,

Julie's Sushi

Degree of Difficulty: Moderately difficult

Sushi artistry as you know it with freshly unfishy notes you don't. Mock salmon provides a creamy counterpart to snappy cucumber in these bite-sized rolls. Dip in wasabi "soy" sauce and pop, pop, pop them in your mouth.

Julie Cheese:
3/4 cup cashews, soaked
1/4 cup water as needed to loosen while blending
2 tablespoons lemon juice
2 tablespoons tamari
1 clove garlic
1/2 teaspoon black pepper

The Meat:
2 cups carrot pulp only from juice
1/4 cup yellow onions
1/4 cup fresh dill, minced
2 teaspoons ginger root
1 teaspoon Kelp Powder
1/2 teaspoon sea salt (to taste)
1 clove garlic
2 teaspoons tamari

Roll it!
4 sheets nori
1 jalapeño pepper
1 tomato
1 cucumber
1 portobello mushroom
1 avocado

Procedure

1. Make Julie's Cheese by blending all cheese ingredients together until smooth. Add water as necessary to keep blender blades moving but this should be pretty thick.
2. Juice enough carrots to create 2 cups of carrot pulp (ideally with a twin gear juicer).
3. In the food processor, rough chop garlic clove, ginger root, packed dill and onion
4. In a bowl, mix Julie's Cheese with carrot pulp, chopped dill mixture, salt and kelp.
5. In a sheet of nori, place 1/4 cup sushi meat on the bottom, press relatively flat in a rectangle 1 inch by 4 inches and form a valley in the center for your veggies.
6. Thinly slice cucumber, portobello, tomato, avocado and jalapeño. Roll. Cut in 6-8 pieces.
7. Serve with a bit of tamari or Braggs Liquid Aminos

Oven Temperature: 105°F

Recipe Tips

** When you mix the Julie's Cheese into the carrot mixture, you can expect to think you won't have enough Cheese. Never fear - you have enough. Work the cheese through with a spatula to force that carrot to incorporate into the cheese.
** If you have a Pampered Chef small ice cream scoop, you can use 5 scoops for each nori roll.

Review

I really loved the sushi. It looked beautiful. I've made raw vegan sushi a few times at home and it's never looked like a neat professional tasty piece of art like this did. The consistency was perfect and the taste was delicious. - Jackie, Staten Island, NY
I have missed sushi so much since I went veg 3.5 years ago. This tasted exactly like how I remember it. I really can't believe it was vegan and raw. Will buy this over and over again! It was amazing! - Jessica, Fairhaven, MA
I've been pretty much "vegan" for 6 years, with the exception of an occasional trip to the sushi bar and I have to say, these are a great substitute...I didn't miss the fish at all. Very flavorful with the nutritional benefit of the nori-Kind of like a California roll, but with more "oomph!" My chopsticks were happy! - Jenni, Minneapolis, MN

Lasagna

Degree of Difficulty: Moderately difficult

4 zucchini
2 tablespoons extra virgin olive oil
1 tablespoon Italian seasoning
4-6 roma tomatoes, sliced
The Red Sauce:
2 cups tomatoes
1 cup sun-dried tomatoes, soaked
1/4 cup yellow onions
1/4 teaspoon crushed red pepper

The Cheese:
2 cups cashews, soaked
1/2 cup water, more if needed
2 tablespoons nutritional yeast
1 tablespoon lemon juice

The Pesto:
1 cup basil, fresh
1 cup parsley, de-stemmed
1/2 cup pistachios
3 tablespoons extra virgin olive oil
1 teaspoon sea salt
1/2 teaspoon black pepper

Procedure

1. Peel zucchini and slice lengthwise in a food processor with a #2 blade or on a 1.5 mm mandolin. Reserve peels if organic.
2. Marinate zucchini with olive oil and Italian seasoning.
3. Process all red sauce ingredients in the food processor until smooth. Place in a bowl and set aside.
4. Process all cheese ingredients in the food processor until smooth. Place in a bowl and set aside.
5. Process all pesto ingredients in the food processor until smooth. Place in a bowl and set aside.
6. Slice tomatoes into very thin rounds.
7. In a 9x12 pain, cover bottom with zucchini strips
8. Scoop 1/3 marinara on top of the noodles and spread gently, being careful not to disturb underlying noodles.
9. Using a tablespoon, layer 1/3 of the lasagna cheese on top of the marinara.
10. Spread 1/3 of the pesto on top of the lasagna cheese.
11. Top pesto layer with sliced tomatoes.
12. Repeat with two more layers of zucchini, red sauce, cheese and tomatoes for a total of three layers.
13. Refrigerate for an hour to allow flavors to mix.
14. Revel in the awe of your guests! You are a RAWK-star!

Recipe Tips

** When spreading cheese and pesto, use a common tablespoon to spread it. Dip your spoon in hot water to help the components spread without jostling your pasta too much.
** Reserve your zucchini peeling, and marinate them in the leftover olive oil and Italian seasoning from your pasta. Dehydrate them and you'll have the Zucchini Sprinkles referenced in our Caesar Salad recipe - yay!
** This recipe was inspired by Sarma Melngailis of Pure Food & Wine in New York. When I first went raw, I took all of my family to eat at Pure Food and Wine and we were astounded. I think they might have been a bit astounded too with our tribe of rowdy kids taking up the biggest table on the patio. Being surrounded by delicious food and glowing people is an experience not to be missed. Thank you Sarma for inspiring sooo many like me!

Review

By far the best raw lasagna I've tried. It tastes just like the real thing and definitely satisfied my pasta craving. - Antioch, TN

Manicotti

Degree of Difficulty: Moderately difficult

Creamy cashew cheese lovingly folded with spinach and our version of sausage wrapped carefully in special zucchini manicotti shells and topped with smoky chipotle infused roasted red pepper sauce.

1 zucchini, peeled, cut in long strips with a mandolin at 1.5 mm
1/2 cup spinach
1 teaspoon sea salt (to taste)

The Sausage:
1/2 cup walnuts
1 cup portobello mushrooms, chopped
3 dates, soaked
1 tablespoon basil, fresh
1/4 teaspoon fennel seeds
1/4 teaspoon sea salt
1/4 teaspoon oregano, dried
1/4 teaspoon black pepper freshly ground
1/8 teaspoon crushed red pepper

The Cheese:
2 cups cashews, soaked
1/2 cup water, more if needed
2 tablespoons nutritional yeast
1 tablespoon lemon juice

Manicotti Sauce
1/2 cup tomatoes, chopped
1/2 cup sun-dried tomatoes
1 red bell pepper
1/4 cup red onions, diced
1/2 cup water as needed
2-3 cloves garlic
1 date
1/2 chipotle pepper, soaked

Procedure

Make the Sausage

1. Process the walnuts till ground rice texture.
2. Add mushrooms, pitted date, fennel, basil, oregano, red pepper flakes, salt and pepper and process to oatmeal like texture - NOT pasty.
3. Roll into links about half inch thick and dehydrate till crispy on the outside and soft inside.

Make The Cheese

Blend all cheese ingredients together until smooth. Place in a glass bowl and set aside.
Make the Sauce:
Blend all sauce ingredients together until smooth. Place in a bowl and set aside.

Assembly

1. Gently combine cheese, spinach and sausage, folding until well incorporated but not mixed. Fold - don't mix.
2. Peel zucchini and slice lengthwise thinly on the mandolin at 1.5 mm
3. Lay 3 slices of zucchini on the cutting board slightly overlapping to create one manicotti noodle.
4. Use small ice cream scoop and place 2-3 scoops of cheese at one edge of the noodle.
5. Roll to make a large manicotti noodle. Place on a serving platter.
6. Repeat to utilize the remaining cheese mixture.
7. Drizzle sauce across the center of the noodles.

Review

These were truly delicious and they look beautiful too. The sauce is packed separately so the zucchini doesn't get soggy. I purchased the individual serving (2 manicotti) and I will definitely order a larger batch next time. It's a really nice sub for the traditional dish.
- S. Nelson, St. Paul, MN

Too spicy for my sweetie: but I thought they were delish! - JA Smith, Marcellus, MI

Mariachi Beet Wrap

Degree of Difficulty: Moderately difficult

From the beet comes a vividly colored wrap fairly bursting with good stuff! There's definitely a Mexican vibe going on: The beet/onion/nut filling is seasoned with cumin, oregano and cayenne, while the collard leaf has tortilla attitude.

1 romaine lettuce or bunch of collard leaves
1 medium beet
1/2 cup almonds
1/2 cup sunflower seeds
1/2 cup red onions
1/4 cup lemon juice
1 tablespoon oregano, dried
1 tablespoon extra virgin olive oil
2 teaspoons Italian seasoning
1-1/2 teaspoons cumin
1/2 teaspoon sea salt
1/4 teaspoon cayenne

Procedure

1. Rough chop beets and onions in food processor.
2. Add remaining ingredient and pulse chop in food processor until a rough falafel texture is achieved.
3. Put a healthy dollop of the beet mixture in a romaine or collard leaf.
4. Shake your mariachi of YUM for the rest of the day.

Recipe Tips

** This recipe came from my fantabulous group of ladies who got together with me once a month to make raw dishes. Kellee brought this and I was hesitant to even try it because I SERIOUSLY dislike beets. But true to raw "uncooking", the real flavors of the beets shines through this dish and makes a truly crave-worthy faux burrito. Thank you, Kellee!!

This has good flavor and I love beets. However, be prepared to add your own salsa, etc.. because it is a lot of filling and not much else. - Angela, NY

Mexi Wrap

Degree of Difficulty: Easy

A pretty romaine wrap is the vessel for diced avocado, tomato and green olive. Cashews and ready-rich macadamia nuts get spun into a creamy dressing fired with jalapeño. Stuff in your own veggies for a feistier fiesta.

1 head romaine hearts or butter lettuce
1 avocado, diced
1 tomato, diced
1/2 cup green olives, diced

The "Spicy Mayo" Part:
1/2 cup water
1 cup cashews, pieces
1/4 jalapeño pepper, minced (leave seeds for more heat)
1 tablespoon nutritional yeast
1 teaspoon lemon juice
1 teaspoon apple cider vinegar
1/2 teaspoon tamari
1/4 teaspoon cumin
1/4 teaspoon coriander
1 garlic clove, minced
pinch of cayenne pepper
sea salt (to taste)

Procedure

1. Put all Spicy Mayo ingredients in the blender and blend till smooth.
2. Dice avocado, tomatoe and olives.
3. Slather some Spicy Mayo on a romaine or collard leaf or a piece of butter lettuce.
4. Place a healthy dollop of avocado mixture on the Mayo
5. Roll up and be prepared to lick your lips.

Review

I loved this dish! The spicy mayo dressing 5 stars, the avocado/olive mix 5 stars. I would order this again! - C. Carree, Gulf Breeze, FL

Pad Thai

Degree of Difficulty: Easy

The sauce makes this dish. It also is very filling. You feel like you are eating a lot of food.
- Angela, NY 1/24/2011

3 cups spiralized zucchini

The Sauce:
3 pitted dates, soaked, reserve water
1/4 cup sun-dried tomatoes, soaked
2 tablespoons Cashew Butter
1 tablespoon lime Juice
1/2 jalapeño pepper, seeded
2 cloves garlic
1/2 inch ginger root
1/2 teaspoon Kelp Powder
1/2 teaspoon apple cider vinegar
1/4 teaspoon sea salt

The Toppings:
1/2 cup red bell peppers, julienned
1/4 cup topping cilantro
1/2 cup portobello mushrooms, sliced
1/3cup red onions

Procedure
Make the Sauce:
1. Blend all sauce ingredients in Vitamix until smooth. Use soak water from dates and sun-dried tomatoes to keep blender blades moving or loosen sauce to desired consistency.
2. Spiralize zucchini.
3. Toss zucchini pasta with sauce.
4. Top with The Toppings.
5. Serve.

Recipe Tips
Being a life-long Midwestern eater meant that I was definitely NOT an adventurous eater. I came from a part of the country where ketchup is considered spicy by many. When I discovered living food, there were many dishes that I simply had never tried in their cooked form but there was some desire for among my friends and family. This is one of those. To this day, I have never had traditional Pad Thai. A huge thank you goes out to my dear friends, Greg & Kellee for putting up with so many different version of "Like this?" and "Change it how?", "More of what?" and on and on and on. You are my inspiration!

The sauce makes this dish. It also is very filling. You feel like you are eating a lot of food.
- Angela, NY

Pasta Bolognese

Degree of Difficulty: Moderately difficult

Fresh zucchini pasta topped with a chunky meaty (though with no meat of course) sauce that will take you back to your fondest thoughts of Italian food - now guilt-free!

3 cups zucchini, spiralized
1/4 cup carrots, shredded

Sausage
1 cup portobello mushrooms, chopped
1/2 cup walnuts
3 dates, soaked
1 tablespoon basil, fresh
1/4 teaspoon fennel seeds
1/4 teaspoon sea salt
1/4 teaspoon oregano, dried
1/4 teaspoon black pepper
1/8 teaspoon pepper flakes

Bolognese Sauce
3 cups tomatoes
1 portobello mushroom
1 avocado
1 cup sun-dried tomatoes, soaked, reserve soak water
1 red bell pepper
1/2 cup cashews
3 tablespoons extra virgin olive oil
2 tablespoons oregano, dried
1 tablespoon dried basil
1 tablespoon tamari
1 teaspoon onion powder
1 teaspoon rosemary
1 teaspoon sea salt
1 teaspoon black pepper
1/2 jalapeño pepper
4-6 cloves garlic

Procedure

Make The Sausage:

1. Process the walnuts till ground rice texture in the food processor.
2. Add remaining sausage ingredients and pulse chop in the food processor. * Should have a slightly chunky texture.
3. Roll into links about half inch thick and dehydrate till crispy on the outside and soft inside, about 6 hours or overnight.
4. Cut into rounds

Make the Sauce

Blend all ingredients till smooth, use reserve soak water if necessary to keep the blender blades moving.

Make the Pasta

1. Spiralize zucchini.
2. Toss zucchini with sauce.
3. Shred carrot.
4. Toss pasta with a healthy portion of sauce.
5. Sprinkle with shredded carrot and sausage to taste.

Recipe Tips

** Leftover sausage and sauce can be frozen for later use.

** This recipe is the creation of a chef we were blessed to have in our kitchen, Tony Delaney. His expertise is BBQ (yes with real meat!) but this dish leaves no doubt that his skills go far beyond the grill and the smoker.

Review

This is one of the family favorites: we like the noodles and sauce (the meaty crumbles are too spicy). Excellent flavor - good family dish - JA Smith, Marcellus, MI

Pepperoni Pizza

Degree of Difficulty: Moderately difficult

You can't mess this one up. Start with our pizza crust, slather on some sauce, toss on those Raw Pepperonis, top with the Mozz cheese. Like the alternative, an instant favorite!

The Crust:
6 cups butternut squash
2 cups walnuts
2 cups golden flaxseed, ground
1/2 cup extra virgin olive oil
1/2 cup red onion
1/4 cup lemon juice
2 tablespoons basil
2 tablespoons nutritional yeast
1 tablespoon oregano, dried
1 teaspoon sea salt

The Sauce:
1 cup tomatoes, diced
1/2 cup sun-dried tomatoes, soaked
1 tablespoon basil, fresh
1 teaspoon oregano, dried
2 cloves garlic, or to taste
1/2 teaspoon sea salt

The Mozz:
2 cups cashews, soaked
1/2 cup water, more if needed
2 tablespoons nutritional yeast
1 tablespoon lemon juice

The Pepperoni:
2 cups zucchini, peeled
1/2 cup almonds, soaked
1/2 red bell pepper seeded & cut into 1/4-inch cubes
1 date
1 teaspoon black pepper
1 teaspoon mustard seed
1 teaspoon fennel seeds
1 teaspoon pepper flakes
1 teaspoon sea salt
1 teaspoon paprika
1/4 teaspoon garlic, powder
1/8 teaspoon liquid smoke

Procedure

Make the Crust:

1. Grind flax and place in bowl.
2. Process all remaining ingredients in food processor until smooth and combine with ground flax.
3. Spread dough to desired pizza size on a teflex sheet and dehydrate for 6 hours.
4. Flip crust and dehydrate for another 12 hours for a crispy crust, 6-8 hours for a softer hand-tossed crust.

Make the Pepperoni

1. In food processor, grind the almonds to just slightly larger than rice size. Remove to mixing bowl.
2. Process zucchini, red pepper, and date till smooth.
3. Mix with ground almonds till a thick falafel-like paste forms.
4. Fold in all remaining ingredients.
5. Drop a tablespoon of the batter on teflex with a small ice cream scoop and flatten slightly to form rounds about the size of a slice of pepperoni.
6. Dehydrate for 12 hours at 105 degrees until crispy, dehydrate for 6-8 hours for softer pepperoni.

Make the Sauce:

Blend together tomatoes, oregano, garlic, and basil with just enough soak water to make a thick sauce.

Make the Cheese

Process all ingredients in the food processor until smooth. Add water as necessary.

The Creation

1. Spread pizza sauce on the crust.
2. Top pizza sauce with the Mozz, use a spoon dipped in hot water to help spread the cheese if it has thickened.
3. Layer Pepperoni Bites on top of the Mozz.
4. Add whatever other fresh toppings your heart desires.

Recipe Tips

** The pizza sauce here is so simple and wonderful! It was created by one of our amazing employees, Cameron. He wasn't with us long but he definitely made a huge impact. Thanks for being a part of our journey, Cameron!

Pineapple Slaw

Degree of Difficulty: Easy

Is there really a way to eat sweet potatoes that doesn't involve Thanksgiving and marshmallows? There is, praise be the beta carotene! This perky slaw is pineapple, Granny Smith apples, pecans and raisin confetti, and just that fun.

3 cups small sweet potatoes, peeled, shredded
1 granny smith apple
1/2 pineapple
1/2 cup pecans
1/4 cup raisins
1 tablespoon lemon juice

Procedure

1. Shred sweet potato and apple with the shredding attachment for the food processor. Place in a glass bowl and set aside.
2. Pulse chop pineapple in the food processor. Add to sweet potato.
3. Toss with rough chopped pecans and raisins and the juice of 1 lemon.

Recipe Tips

** You'll believe me now if I tell you I don't like sweet potatoes? My friend, Mona, part of our Raw Ladies Group introduced me to this wonderful little dish. She brought me this treat after one of my babies was born and it was dressed with Veganaise. I just left that off and voila! an easy peasy treat that takes 5 minutes to make and keeps you full all day. AND now I like sweet potatoes and I LOVE Mona!!

Review

This is the most tasty, sweet and refreshing slaw that I have ever had! I actually like that it doesn't have cabbage. - T. Baklund, Dassel, MN

As a newbie to raw foods, this was really a treat. Both taste and texture were just right. It was fresh and crisp, with mild sweetness, while the addition of the pecans made it hearty without weighing you down. Highly recommend! - Grace, El Paso, TX

Yummy. Sweet, acidic with a little crunch. This is a great side. - J. Anderson, Lubbock, TX

Pineapple Sweet & Sour

Degree of Difficulty: Easy

Classic Pure Market Express "rice" topped with a variety of yummy fresh veggies and topped with a delightful sweet and sour pineapple sauce will give you everything you need to finish your day strong!

The Rice:
1 cup cashews
1 cup parsnips
Sweet & Sour Sauce:
1/2 cup agave nectar
1/2 cup pineapple
1/3 cup cashews
1/4 cup red onions
1 inch ginger
2 tablespoons tamari
1 tablespoon ume plum vinegar
3 cloves garlic

The Goodies:
1 cup broccoli, rough chopped
1/2 cup carrots, sliced into rounds
1 red bell pepper, julienned
1/2 cup pineapple, diced

Procedure

Make the Sauce:
1. Rice: Place parsnips in food processor until rice grain size. Add cashews and process to rice consistency.
2. Cut vegetables and toss with rice.
3. Blend sauce ingredients until smooth, toss with rice mixture.

Recipe Tips
** Another fabulous creation by Tony Delaney. Sometimes CraigsList serves up a true treasure! That's how we found Tony and he definitely left his mark on Pure Market Express.

Review
5 stars is just not enough to show how great the pineapple sweet and sour is. Crunchy, chewy, sweet, and sour all in one. I love food and think it should be exciting. Nothing boring with this dish. Yum, yum, yum! - J. Greene, Winter Haven, FL
This has to be one of my favorite dishes!! I didn't even care that I ate both servings (which I didn't realize until AFTER I ate everything LOL). - S. Robertson, Cordova, TN
Family Favorite - we were skeptical about parsnip "rice" but loved loved, loved this dish. Wish we could buy the sauce for noodle dishes as well. - JA Smith, Marcellus, MI

Quinoa Tabouli

Degree of Difficulty: Easy

Enjoy straight from the fridge on a bed of romaine for a supercharged lunch that prepares you to take on the rest of the day!

1 cup quinoa, sprouted (can sub hemp seeds)
1/2 cup tomatoes, chopped
1/4 cup parsley, minced
1/2 cup red bell peppers, diced
1/4 cup red onions
1 cup cucumbers, chopped
1 tablespoon extra virgin olive oil
1 tablespoon lemon juice
1 teaspoon Kelp Powder
1 teaspoon tamari
Salt and freshly ground pepper, to taste

Procedure

1. Measure and soak quinoa in 3 cups warm water for at least 1 hour, overnight if you want it to sprout.
2. Dice tomatoes, parsley, green pepper, green onion, and cucumber in the dicer.
3. Mix oil and lemon juice together and sprinkle with kelp powder and tamari for dressing.
4. Drain and rinse quinoa and toss with veggies and dressing.

Recipe Tips

** Try using hemp seed in place of the quinoa for a fabulous high protein lunch!

Ravioli

Degree of Difficulty: Easy

The most delicate dish on our menu, our ravioli is art for the eye, a personal party for you. Paper-thin turnip rounds contain a cheesy, nutty filling with echoes of red bell pepper and fresh basil. Pillows glisten with garlic-infused olive oil.

2 medium turnips, sliced paper thin, need at least 24 slices
1/4 cup extra virgin olive oil
1 teaspoon minced garlic
1/4 cup basil, chiffonade

The Red Pepper Cheeze:
1-1/2 cups cashews, soaked
1/2 red bell pepper
1/4 cup tamari
1 tablespoon nutritional yeast

Procedure

1. Blend olive oil and garlic to create an infusion.
2. Brush a serving plate with garlic extra virgin olive oil.
3. For red pepper cheeze, combine all ingredients in the Vitamix and blend until smooth.
4. Slice turnips thinly on the mandolin. Cut circles with a cookie cutter approximately 2 inches round
5. Lay 12 turnip slices on the serving plate. Take another 12 turnip slices and cut a small pie shaped piece out of each.
6. Place 1-2 teaspoons of filling on the turnip circles and top with a pie piece turnip slice, folding it so it creates a tiny hat over the cheeze.
7. Top with a drizzle of olive oil and a sprinkle of basil chiffonade.

Recipe Tips

** Leftover cheeze can be frozen for future use.

Review

This was the first entree item that I tried, and it was scrumptious and quite filling.
- E. Wald, Okemos, MI

This was the first entree I tried as well - because it looked so delicious and tasty. It was... absolutely amazing! Great presentation and wonderfully delicious filling. The texture of the filling was so creamy - I wish I could come close to making something like this myself. And the garlic bread had an amazing flavor. I am tempted to buy a package of nothing but ravioli after eating this. - Beth, Richardson, TX

I loved the flavor of these delicate ravioli--I did not find the garlic overpowering at all. I especially enjoyed the bell pepper "cheese" filling.
- S. Nelson, St. Paul, MN

Red Pepper Corn Salsa

Degree of Difficulty: Easy

As simple as salsa, red peppers, corn, tomato, cilantro, onion, jalapeño pepper and sea salt. This spicy combination is an enjoyable side just waiting to be dipped.

2 cups corn
1 cup tomato, diced
1 cup red belesl peppers, diced
1/2 cup red onions, diced
1/4 cup cilantro, minced
1/2 jalapeño pepper, minced
1/2 teaspoon sea salt (to taste)

Procedure

1. Dice bell peppers, tomatoes, onions, and jalapeño pepper.
2. Mince cilantro.
3. Toss diced ingredients, minced cilantro, corn and salt.

Salmon & Hollandaise

Degree of Difficulty: Easy

Is a fillet without the fish still worthy of being called seafood? The addition of seaweed (kelp) to this recipe gives it all the ocean credibility it needs. Using carrot as the base ingredient works swimmingly—you'll see.

Julie Cheese:
3/4 cup cashews, soaked
1/4 cup water, as needed to loosen while blending
2 tablespoons lemon juice
2 tablespoons tamari
1 clove garlic
1/2 teaspoon black pepper

The Meat:
2 cups carrot pulp only from juice
1/4 cup yellow onions
1/4 cup fresh dill, minced
2 teaspoons ginger root
1 teaspoon Kelp Powder
1/2 teaspoon sea salt (to taste)
1 clove garlic
2 teaspoons tamari

Hollandaise Sauce
1 avocado, over-ripe
1/4 cup extra virgin olive oil
1 tablespoon lemon juice
2 teaspoons turmeric
1/2 teaspoon sea salt
1/8 teaspoon cayenne
water as needed to loosen while blending
1/2 cup almonds, soaked

Procedure

1. Make Julie's Cheese by blending all cheese ingredients together until smooth. Add water as necessary to keep blender blades moving but this should be pretty thick.
2. Juice enough carrots to create 2 cups of carrot pulp (ideally with a twin gear juicer).
3. In the food processor, rough chop garlic clove, ginger root, packed dill and onion.
4. In a bowl, mix Julie's Cheese with carrot pulp, chopped dill mixture, salt and kelp.
5. Take 1/2-3/4 cup of the salmon mixture and form into a fishy shape. Place in the dehydrator at 105 degrees for 30-60 minutes until the salmon turns a darker orange salmon color and gets crispy on the outside.
6. Blend all hollandaise ingredients until smooth.
7. Drizzle hollandaise over the warm salmon or use the hollandaise as a dipping sauce.

Recipe Tips

** When you mix the Julie's Cheese into the carrot mixture, you can expect to think you won't have enough Cheese. Never fear - you have enough. Work the cheese through with a spatula to force that carrot to incorporate into the cheese.

Sausage Pizza

Degree of Difficulty: Moderately difficult

Pizza pizzazz is yours with our four-step assembly. Crust? Check. Tomato sauce? Yes. Mozzarella? Affirmative. Sausage? Of course. Delicious? Mama Mia!

The Crust:
6 cups butternut squash
2 cups walnuts
2 cups golden flaxseed, ground
1/2 cup extra virgin olive oil
1/2 cup red onions
1/4 cup lemon juice
2 tablespoons basil
2 tablespoons nutritional yeast
1 tablespoon oregano, dried
1 teaspoon sea salt

The Sauce:
1 cup tomatoes, diced
1/2 cup sun-dried tomatoes, soaked
1 tablespoon basil, fresh
1 teaspoon oregano, dried
2 cloves garlic, or to taste
1/2 teaspoon sea salt

The Mozz:
2 cups cashews, soaked
1/2 cup water, more if needed
2 tablespoons nutritional yeast
1 tablespoon lemon juice

Sausage
1 cup portobello mushrooms, chopped
1/2 cup walnuts
3 dates, soaked
1 tablespoon basil, fresh
1/4 teaspoon fennel seeds
1/4 teaspoon sea salt
1/4 teaspoon oregano, dried
1/4 teaspoon black pepper
1/8 teaspoon pepper flakes

Procedure

1. Grind flax and place in bowl.
2. Process all remaining ingredients in food processor until smooth and combine with ground flax.
3. Spread dough to desired pizza size on a teflex sheet and dehydrate for 6 hours.
4. Flip crust and dehydrate for another 12 hours for a crispy crust, 6-8 hours for a softer hand-tossed crust.

Make the Sausage

1. Process the walnuts till ground rice texture in the food processor.
2. Add remaining ingredients and pulse chop in the food processor. * Should have a slightly chunky texture.
3. Roll into links about half inch thick and dehydrate till crispy on the outside and soft inside, about 6 hours or overnight.
4. Cut into rounds for pizza and gnosh!

Make the Sauce

Blend together tomatoes, oregano, garlic, and basil with just enough soak water to make a thick sauce.

Make the Cheese

Process all ingredient in the food processor until smooth. Add water as necessary.

The Creation

1. Spread pizza sauce on the crust.
2. Top pizza sauce with the Mozz, use a spoon dipped in hot water to help spread the cheese if it has thickened.
3. Layer sausage on top of the Mozz.
4. Add whatever other fresh toppings your heart desires.

Oven Temperature: 105°F

Spanish Rice

Degree of Difficulty: Easy

Hereby proving that comfort food comes in many packages, our Spanish rice satisfies at that level.

The Rice:
1 cup parsnips, peeled
1 cup cashews

Spicy Lentil Taco Meat - 1/2 cup

Sassy Salsa - 1 cup

The Spanish Sauce:
1/4 cup sun-dried tomatoes, soaked (reserve soak water)
1/4 cup yellow onions
1/4 jalapeño pepper, seeded and diced
1 clove garlic, minced
2 tablespoons extra virgin olive oil
2 teaspoons lime juice
1/2 teaspoon oregano
1/4 teaspoon sea salt
1/8 teaspoon chili powder
1/8 teaspoon black pepper
1/8 teaspoon cumin

Procedure
1. Pulse parsnips and cashews until mixture resembles rice. Place in a bowl and set aside.
2. Blend all remaining ingredients EXCEPT Salsa and Taco Meat to create a sauce.
3. Toss rice with sauce mixture.
4. Fold Sassy Salsa and Spicy Lentil Taco Meat into the rice mixture until completely incorporated.
5. Dive in!

Reviews
I will definitely order this one again. I just loved the spice and flavor and texture. Really flavorful and fresh! - S. Nelson, St. Paul, MN 7/18/2012
Blown away! I could not believe how much this tasted like the real thing. So good I cursed. - J. Kerrine, Silver Spring, MD 11/11/2012

Spicy Peanut Pasta

Degree of Difficulty: Easy

The Pasta:
3 cups spiralized zucchini

Spicy Peanut Sauce
1/4 cup sun-dried tomatoes
1/4 jalapeño pepper
1/2 inch ginger root, fresh, minced
1 clove garlic
2 tablespoons tamari
2 tablespoons Cashew Butter water as needed to loosen while blending

Procedure
1. Spiralize approximately 2 zucchinis.
2. Blend all sauce ingredients until smooth.
3. Toss with zucchini pasta.

Review
I will be honest, I don't like zucchini but this was the best thing I have ever had!!! It doesn't even taste like zucchini! Oh it was so yummy:) - S. Jenkins, Titusville, FL
The garlic alfredo sauce was incredibly creamy and flavorful. - Jessica

Stir Fry-less

Degree of Difficulty: Easy

We stir a complex sauce into a farmers' market stand of nine vegetables plus garlic, gingerroot and herbs. The resulting sauce could not, honestly, be more flavorful for your home raw stir fry~

1 carrot, shredded
1 zucchini, shredded
1/4 head purple cabbage, shredded
1 small parsnip, shredded
1 red bell pepper, julienned
1 cup broccoli, rough chopped
1/2 cup red onions, minced
1/2 cup parsley
1/4 cup sesame seed

The Sauce:
1/2 cup extra virgin olive oil
2 teaspoons ume plum vinegar
2 teaspoons tamari
2 cloves garlic
1/2 inch ginger root, minced

Procedure
1. Shred carrot, zucchini, cabbage, and parsnips in with the shredder attachment to your food processor and place in a mixing bowl.
2. Julienne red bell pepper, chop broccoli and parsley and toss with minced red onions.
3. Toss all ingredients with sesame seed.
4. Blend ume plum vinegar, tamari, olive oil, and ginger till smooth.
5. Toss with veggies. Let marinate for at least 30 minutes for veggies to soften.
6. YUM!

Taco Salad

Degree of Difficulty: Easy

2 cups romaine lettuce, chopped
1 avocado, diced
1 tomato, diced
1/4 cup Spicy Lentil Taco Meat
1 cup Mexi Chips
1/4 cup Sour Cream

Procedure

1. Chop 2 cups romaine lettuce. Place on a large plate.
2. Crumble Corn Chips on top of the romaine.
3. Dice avocado and tomato and toss with Spicy Lentil Taco Meat.
4. Spread a healthy layer of the meat and salsa mixture over the crumbled chips.
5. Top with a dollop of Sour Cream and dig in.

Thai Salad

Degree of Difficulty: Easy

Think chopped salad meets Thai pantry. Cabbage, red bell pepper, cilantro, mint, bean sprouts, green onion and curried cashews in creamy, sesame-lime dressing make for a bright, snappy Southeast Asian taste jaunt.

4 cups romaine lettuce
2 cups purple cabbage, shredded
1 red bell pepper, julienned
1/2 cup sundried tomatoes, soaked, chiffonade
1/2 cup cilantro, minced
2 teaspoons mint

Creamy Thai Dressing
3 tablespoons cashews
3 tablespoons extra virgin olive oil
2 tablespoons tamari
1 tablespoon hemp oil
1 tablespoon lime juice
1 tablespoon maple syrup
1/4 inch ginger root
1 teaspoon crushed red chili peppers
Salt and freshly ground black pepper to taste

Procedure

1. Blend all sauce ingredients till smooth.
2. Combine all salad ingredients
3. Toss with Dressing
4. Eat.

Turkey Salad Wrap

Degree of Difficulty: Easy

A fresh light salad, spiced with sage; bring this to your picnic and impress.

1 head romaine hearts, collards or butter lettuce
1 cup cashews
1 cup pumpkin seeds
1/2 cup Brazil nuts
5 stalks celery
1/4 cup yellow onions
1 teaspoon sage
1/2 teaspoon sea salt

Procedure

1. Process all ingredients except lettuce until roughly chopped.
2. Place approximately 1/2 cup of the turkey mixture in a lettuce wrap and gnosh!

garlic crackers
corn chips
Crackers Chips & Cereal
pizza chips

CHEESE! Omigosh I love cheese! Always have since I was a little kid. When I went raw, I had to have, and I do mean HAD TO have, cheese. It took me a long time and many, many messy days in the kitchen to figure these out but now I can say again I LOVE CHEESE!

Okay one of the best things about raw vegan cheese is that it can be frozen. So you can spend a lovely afternoon playing and creating all kinds of different varieties and pop them in the freezer for later use. Alternatively, I would encourage you to make a larger batch of cheese base and freeze that in 2 or 3 cup portions so you can make fresh cheese whenever you please.

Raw vegan cheese will be a loose spread when it is finished but it will thicken nicely in the refrigerator or freezer. Now there are amazing techniques to make hard cheeses as well. I am super inspired by that but honestly I just get too impatient! Play with these recipes. I used to hunt online cheese forums and get flavor combination ideas from them to see if could recreate them at home. Fun!

Cheddar Cheese

Degree of Difficulty: Easy

A whipped base of cashews puts the spreader in the cheddar, while rich flavor comes compliments of sun-dried tomatoes, bell pepper, lemon and garlic. Sound the call for crackers!

Cheese Base
4 cups water
2 cups cashews, pieces
1/8 teaspoon acidophilus

The Red Pepper Cheeze:
1-1/2 cups cashews, soaked
1/2 red bell pepper
1/4 cup tamari
1 tablespoon nutritional yeast

Procedure

1. Soak cashews in 4 cups warm water for at least one hour. Drain and rinse.
2. Blend all ingredients till smooth.

Recipe Tips

** Place the red pepper at the bottom of the blender carafe to assist the blades in moving.
** Cheddar Cheese will thicken in the refrigerator. Store in the refrigerator for up to 14 days.
** Can be frozen for later use.

Review

This was a delicious cheese that we tried on the chili lime "bread." I thought they complimented each other perfectly. This cheese could be used for any type of Mexican food and just tastes phenomenal. You can hardly notice a difference and the texture is true to a spreadable cheese. - A. Abercrombie, Minneapolis, MN

Chipotle Garlic Cheese

Degree of Difficulty: Easy

Smoky chipotle and fresh garlic marry up to combine this flavor sensation.

Cheese Base
4 cups water
2 cups cashews, pieces
1/8 teaspoon acidophilus

Chipotle Garlic Seasoning
4 cloves garlic (more as you please)
1 chipotle pepper, soaked
1 teaspoon sea salt

Procedure
Cheese Base

1. Put 4 cups of water in a glass bowl.
2. Add cashews. If you have whole cashews, you will want to break them up into large pieces to encourage fermentation
3. Add 1/8 teaspoon of vegan acidophilus.
4. Cover bowl loosely with cheesecloth for approximately 48 hours.
5. When done, you will see bubbles rising to the top of the bowl and the liquid will look thick.
6. Strain liquid into a separate bowl. Reserve soak liquid.
7. Place cashews in the Vitamix and blend till smooth. Add soak water as necessary to keep the blades moving.
8. Cheese will be loose when finished.

Now add your yummy seasonings! - Fold in and refrigerate for 6-8 hours to set.

Recipe Tips

** Try using hemp seed in place of the quinoa for a fabulous high protein lunch!

Cilantro Jalapeño Cheese

Degree of Difficulty: Easy

Make mine Mexican. This is "the" cheese for corn chips, tacos, tostadas, fajitas and more. Lime juice, cumin, cayenne: The cha-cha-cha is here, here, here.

Cheese Base
4 cups water
2 cups cashews, pieces
1/8 teaspoon acidophilus

The Cilantro Jalapeño Part:
1/2 cup cilantro, chopped
1/2 jalapeño pepper, minced (leave seeds for more heat)
3 tablespoons nutritional yeast
1 teaspoon sea salt

Procedure
Cheese Base

1. Put 4 cups of water in a glass bowl.
2. Add cashews. If you have whole cashews, you will want to break them up into large pieces to encourage fermentation
3. Add 1/8 teaspoon of vegan acidophilus.
4. Cover bowl loosely with cheesecloth for approximately 48 hours.
5. When done, you will see bubbles rising to the top of the bowl and the liquid will look thick.
6. Strain liquid into a separate bowl. Reserve soak liquid.
7. Place cashews in the Vitamix and blend till smooth. Add soak water as necessary to keep the blades moving.
8. Cheese will be loose when finished.

Now add your yummy seasonings! - Fold in and refrigerate for 6-8 hours to set.

Review

This is the most amazing non-dairy cheese that I have ever had! I enjoyed it thoroughly, not even missing a bit of the dairy- it's creamy, so flavorful, simply awesome! - Tara B., Dassel, MN

Creamy Herb Cheese

Degree of Difficulty: Easy

Serve this flavorful spread with our onion bagels or any of our snappy crackers.

Cheese Base
4 cups water
2 cups cashews, pieces
1/8 teaspoon acidophilus

The Herb Part:
1/2 cup red onions, minced
1 tablespoon Italian seasoning
1 clove garlic, minced
1 teaspoon sea salt

Procedure

Cheese Base

1. Put 4 cups of water in a glass bowl.
2. Add cashews. If you have whole cashews, you will want to break them up into large pieces to encourage fermentation
3. Add 1/8 teaspoon of vegan acidophilus.
4. Cover bowl loosely with cheesecloth for approximately 48 hours.
5. When done, you will see bubbles rising to the top of the bowl and the liquid will look thick.
6. Strain liquid into a separate bowl. Reserve soak liquid.
7. Place cashews in the Vitamix and blend till smooth. Add soak water as necessary to keep the blades moving.
8. Cheese will be loose when finished.

Now add your yummy seasonings!
Fold in and refrigerate for 6-8 hours to set.

Review

Tastes like Boursin! I had no idea how this would taste but it takes like goat cheese with herbs- very authentic. - J. Kerrine, Silver Spring, MD
Outstanding! Great flavor for dressings, chips, crackers, zucchini noodles, anything - creamy herb goodness! - JA Smith, Marcellus, MI

Good as Gouda Cheese

Degree of Difficulty: Easy

Any cracker is better under a swipe of this somewhat edgy, slightly smoky pleasure. With cashews and pine nuts as starting points, our goodly Gouda does away with the "Moo" and makes way for a healthier "Mmm."

Cheese Base
4 cups water
2 cups cashews, pieces
1/8 teaspoon acidophilus

The Goodly Gouda Part:
3 tablespoons nutritional yeast
1/8 teaspoon liquid smoke
1 clove garlic, minced
1 teaspoon sea salt

Procedure

Cheese Base

1. Put 4 cups of water in a glass bowl.
2. Add cashews. If you have whole cashews, you will want to break them up into large pieces to encourage fermentation
3. Add 1/8 teaspoon of vegan acidophilus.
4. Cover bowl loosely with cheesecloth for approximately 48 hours.
5. When done, you will see bubbles rising to the top of the bowl and the liquid will look thick.
6. Strain liquid into a separate bowl. Reserve soak liquid.
7. Place cashews in the Vitamix and blend till smooth. Add soak water as necessary to keep the blades moving.
8. Cheese will be loose when finished.

Now add your yummy seasonings!
Fold in and refrigerate for 6-8 hours to set.

Review

Oh. Em. Gee. I could lick the container clean, this stuff is so good. It's also incredibly filling. I'll definitely order this again. Creamy, smoky, and so delicious. - KL Grady, Virginia Beach, VA

Mexi Cheese

Degree of Difficulty: Easy

Serve this flavorful spread with our onion bagels or any of our snappy crackers.

Cheese Base
4 cups water
2 cups cashews, pieces
1/8 teaspoon acidophilus

The Mexi Part:
1 jalapeño pepper, minced (leave seeds for more heat)
3 tablespoons nutritional yeast
2 tablespoons lemon juice
1 tablespoon apple cider vinegar
4 cloves garlic, minced
2 teaspoons tamari
1 teaspoon sea salt
1 teaspoon cumin
3/4 teaspoon coriander
1/4 teaspoon cayenne pepper

Procedure

Cheese Base

1. Put 4 cups of water in a glass bowl.
2. Add cashews. If you have whole cashews, you will want to break them up into large pieces to encourage fermentation
3. Add 1/8 teaspoon of vegan acidophilus.
4. Cover bowl loosely with cheesecloth for approximately 48 hours.
5. When done, you will see bubbles rising to the top of the bowl and the liquid will look thick.
6. Strain liquid into a separate bowl. Reserve soak liquid.
7. Place cashews in the Vitamix and blend till smooth. Add soak water as necessary to keep the blades moving.
8. Cheese will be loose when finished.

Now add your yummy seasonings!
Fold in and refrigerate for 6-8 hours to set.

PepperJack Cheese

Degree of Difficulty: Easy

Cheese Base
4 cups water
2 cups cashews, pieces
1/8 teaspoon acidophilus

The PepperJack Part:
1/2 jalapeño pepper, minced (leave seeds for more heat)
1/2 teaspoon red pepper flakes
4 cloves garlic, minced
1 teaspoon sea salt

Procedure

Cheese Base

1. Put 4 cups of water in a glass bowl.
2. Add cashews. If you have whole cashews, you will want to break them up into large pieces to encourage fermentation
3. Add 1/8 teaspoon of vegan acidophilus.
4. Cover bowl loosely with cheesecloth for approximately 48 hours.
5. When done, you will see bubbles rising to the top of the bowl and the liquid will look thick.
6. Strain liquid into a separate bowl. Reserve soak liquid.
7. Place cashews in the Vitamix and blend till smooth. Add soak water as necessary to keep the blades moving.
8. Cheese will be loose when finished.

Now add your yummy seasonings!
Fold in and refrigerate for 6-8 hours to set.

Review

I was really hesitant to try this. I am so glad I did. What a rich and filling texture and taste. Dare I say it tastes better than real cheese without the bloating and sleepy feeling afterwards? Who knew raw would taste so good!!! You have a new fan!! - K. Shaddock, Milton, MA

Simply Basil Cheese

Degree of Difficulty: Easy

Serve this flavorful spread with our onion bagels or any of our snappy crackers.

Cheese Base
4 cups water
2 cups cashews, pieces
1/8 teaspoon acidophilus

The Basil Part:
1/2 cup basil, chiffonade
2 tablespoons extra virgin olive oil
1 teaspoon sea salt

Procedure

Cheese Base

1. Put 4 cups of water in a glass bowl.
2. Add cashews. If you have whole cashews, you will want to break them up into large pieces to encourage fermentation
3. Add 1/8 teaspoon of vegan acidophilus.
4. Cover bowl loosely with cheesecloth for approximately 48 hours.
5. When done, you will see bubbles rising to the top of the bowl and the liquid will look thick.
6. Strain liquid into a separate bowl. Reserve soak liquid.
7. Place cashews in the Vitamix and blend till smooth. Add soak water as necessary to keep the blades moving.
8. Cheese will be loose when finished.

Now add your yummy seasonings!
Fold in and refrigerate for 6-8 hours to set.

Spicy Peppercorn Cheese

Degree of Difficulty: Easy

Pity black pepper: It's always in the shadow of salt. This spread invites ground peppercorns to step to the fore and they deliver magnificently. Crackers, sandwiches, raw recipes requiring something more: All find it here.

Cheese Base
4 cups water
2 cups cashews, pieces
1/8 teaspoon acidophilus

The Peppercorn Part:
1/2 cup red onions, minced
4 teaspoons peppercorns (mixed peppercorn blend is especially pretty)
1 teaspoon sea salt

Procedure

Cheese Base

1. Put 4 cups of water in a glass bowl.
2. Add cashews. If you have whole cashews, you will want to break them up into large pieces to encourage fermentation
3. Add 1/8 teaspoon of vegan acidophilus.
4. Cover bowl loosely with cheesecloth for approximately 48 hours.
5. When done, you will see bubbles rising to the top of the bowl and the liquid will look thick.
6. Strain liquid into a separate bowl. Reserve soak liquid.
7. Place cashews in the Vitamix and blend till smooth. Add soak water as necessary to keep the blades moving.
8. Cheese will be loose when finished.

Now add your yummy seasonings!
Fold in and refrigerate for 6-8 hours to set.

Review

This is the first vegan cheese (not to mention raw!) that actually tastes like dairy. It's just perfectly creamy and spicy. This will be a staple for me. - S. Nelson, St. Paul, MN

Tomato Basil Cheese

Degree of Difficulty: Easy

The smooth hails from whirred cashews. The "picnic on the piazza" vibe has its origins in densely flavored tomato and sprightly basil.

2 cups cashews
1/8 tsp vegan acidophilus

The Tomato Basil Part:
3/4 cup sun-dried tomatoes, softened and minced
1/2 cup basil, chiffonade
1 teaspoon sea salt

Procedure
Cheese Base
1. Put 4 cups of water in a glass bowl.
2. Add cashews. If you have whole cashews, you will want to break them up into large pieces to encourage fermentation
3. Add 1/8 teaspoon of vegan acidophilus.
4. Cover bowl loosely with cheesecloth for approximately 48 hours.
5. When done, you will see bubbles rising to the top of the bowl and the liquid will look thick.
6. Strain liquid into a separate bowl. Reserve soak liquid.
7. Place cashews in the Vitamix and blend till smooth. Add soak water as necessary to keep the blades moving.
8. Cheese will be loose when finished.

Now add your yummy seasonings!
Fold in and refrigerate for 6-8 hours to set.

Review
I should have known better than to not have high expectations, but I have made raw cheeses before at home and found that they were just too heavy for me. This on the other hand was light and delicious. I was expecting a raw cheese with a tomato here and a tiny spec of basil there, but this was bursting with yumminess! This would impress any cheese lover. Went great on the BBQ thins (thanks for the suggestion Rebecca!)
- Tanya, Newport, MN

This has to be my favorite of all the cheeses I've tried so far. It is soooo good. Will definitely stay on my rotation! - S. Robertson, Cordova, TN

This cheese is soooo yummy. It's more the consistency of a cream cheese than some others I've tried. It is very salty so be prepared for that.
- Gentry, AR

Seriously Good Components

Here we have the "faux" recipes. No matter how healthy I get – these things I still crave. And more than that, I found that adding a seriously good component can make a recipe, take it to a whole new level and really make it seriously CRAVE-worthy. Garlic Alfredo Pasta goes from "Oh yes that's good" to "Oh. Em. Gee. That is A-mazing!" If you could master the recipes in this section and the cheese base recipe, that would be enough to seriously revolutionize your eating and your health.

Sassy Salsa

Hummus

Bac'Un

Degree of Difficulty: Easy

1 eggplant, peeled.
1/2 teaspoon cayenne
1/4 cup extra virgin olive oil
1/4 cup ume plum vinegar

Procedure

1. Peel eggplant.
2. Slice with the Cuisinart on the #2 blade.
3. Mix cayenne, olive oil and vinegar.
4. Marinate in eggplant for at least 1 hour, tossing once.
5. Dehydrate until crispy.

Hummus

Degree of Difficulty: Easy

Creamy garlicky goodness guilt-free anytime!

2 medium zucchinis
1/2 cup sunflower seeds, ground
1/4 cup lemon juice
4 cloves garlic
2 tablespoons tahini
2 tablespoons extra virgin olive oil
1 teaspoon sea salt
1 teaspoon cumin
1/4 teaspoon cayenne

Procedure

1. Process sunflower seeds into a powder and set aside.
2. Process zucchinis, garlic, lemon juice, olive oil and tahini until smooth.
3. Slowly add in ground sunflower seeds to desired consistency.

Review

Spread the love. Love this zippy hummus as a spread on the Onion Bread w/Bac'Un and lettuce. And the green olive slices brought a complete flavor. - AM Day, Baraboo, MI

Ketchup

Degree of Difficulty: Easy

Tired of ketchup with high fructose corn syrup as a main ingredient? Never fear - now you can whip up your own favorite condiment.

2 cups sun-dried tomatoes
1 cup tomatoes
1/4 cup red onions
4 cloves garlic
2 tablespoons basil, dried
2 tablespoons maple syrup
2 tablespoons extra virgin olive oil
1 tablespoon tamari
3 dates

Procedure

Blend till smooth.

Sassy Salsa

Degree of Difficulty: Moderately difficult

Salsa so fresh, so tasty, so mouthwatering, you can only call it sassy!

3 cups roma tomatoes, diced
1 cup roma tomatoes, pureed
1 bunch cilantro, minced
1/2 red bell pepper, diced
1/2 cup red onions
3 tablespoons lime Juice
2 tablespoons extra virgin olive oil
1 tablespoon garlic powder
2 teaspoons oregano, dried
1/2 seeded jalapeño pepper
3 cloves garlic
1-1/2 teaspoons cumin
3/4 teaspoon sea salt
1/2 teaspoon black pepper
1/4 teaspoon cayenne

Procedure
Dice all ingredients with press and combine.

Recipe Tips
** This recipe is the creation of our first chef, Jacob Schloner. The story still makes me smile. We were working on recipes in my kitchen at home. Jacob was not a raw chef and it was the first of several times over the years to come that I was impressed with the openness of folks who had built their career in meat making skills to learn a whole new discipline. Anyway, I wasn't happy with the salsa recipe I had created so Jacob went to work. Before long he had created the salsa that now passes to you. We all really enjoyed it but my husband said, well we'll have to give it a name for the website. The name came immediately to mind that it was so fresh it was "Sassy" so that's what I said. We'll call it Sassy Salsa. Jacob turned to me with a look of mild horror (and just a glint of humor in his eyes) and said, "You're going to call my salsa SASSY??" I giggled and said, "Yup." And I still smile. Thank you, Jacob, for being a part of the Pure Market Express vision.

Review
Perfect! Living in Texas I have tried a lot of salsa. This is the best hands down. I could eat this with a spoon without the chips. All I can say is the taste is right on hot but not too hot, and just the right amount of cilantro. Perfect. I have already ordered more. - G. Hutchinson, Plano, TX

Sausage

Degree of Difficulty: Easy

1 cup portobello mushrooms, chopped
1/2 cup walnuts
3 dates, soaked
1 tablespoon basil, fresh
1/4 teaspoon fennel seeds
1/4 teaspoon sea salt
1/4 teaspoon oregano, dried
1/4 teaspoon black pepper
1/8 teaspoon pepper flakes

Procedure
1. Process the walnuts till ground rice texture in the food processor.
2. Add remaining ingredients and pulse chop in the food processor. * Should have a slightly chunky texture.
3. Roll into links about half inch thick and dehydrate till crispy on the outside and soft inside, about 6 hours or overnight.

Sour Cream

Degree of Difficulty: Easy

Love cows? Leave the dairy to them! Make your own sour cream that will feed your brain with omega three's!

1 cup Young Thai coconut meat
1/2 cup cashews
1 tablespoon lemon juice
1 teaspoon apple cider vinegar
1/2 teaspoon sea salt
water as needed to loosen while blending

Procedure

1. Drain and trim coconut meat of all brown pieces.
2. Add all ingredients to the blender and blend till smooth. Add water 1 tablespoon at a time just enough to keep the blades moving.
3. Mixture will thicken as it chills.

Spicy Lentil Taco Meat

Degree of Difficulty: Moderately difficult

4 cups carrots, pulp only
2 cups lentils, sprouted
1 cup portobello mushrooms
1 cup yellow onions, peeled and chopped
1/2 cup roma tomatoes
2 tablespoons lime juice
1 tablespoon ground coriander
1 tablespoon cumin
1 tablespoon oregano, dried
2 teaspoons tamari
1/2 teaspoon sea salt
1/2 teaspoon black pepper
1/4 teaspoon chili powder
1/8 teaspoon cayenne
1/2 seeded jalapeño pepper
2-4 cloves garlic

Procedure

1. Soak 1 cup of lentils in 2 cups of warm water for 24 hours or until you see tiny tails on the seeds, usually no longer than 48 hours.
2. Process the sprouted lentils in the food processor on pulse chop. Place in glass bowl.
3. Juice carrots in a twin gear juicer. Drink juice and reserve pulp. Add pulp to lentils.
4. Rough chop onions, mushrooms, tomatoes, garlic and jalapeño pepper in food processor.
5. Combine lentils and onion mixture.
6. Add all remaining ingredients to the bowl and mix by hand until completely incorporated.
7. Place on teflex sheet approximately 1/2 inch thick, not packed or flat. Make it fluffy.
8. Dehydrate for 5-6 hours at 105 degrees. Taco meat should NOT be crunchy. Leave it in just long enough that it turns to a brown hamburger color and is slightly crispy on the outside.
9. * Be very careful with this recipe. It is super easy to over dehydrate. Remove it from the dehydrator as soon as you see the carrots turn to a brown color like ground beef.
10. * If you DO over dry, never fear - you have the best salad topping ever now!

Drinks

Creamy Strawberry Smoothie

Cacao Bean

Brazil nut milk

All right, here is the straight scoop on Pure Market Express Smoothies. Over half of these recipes come straight from our oldest daughter, Rachel, who managed the entire kitchen from 2010 through 2012. She really has a gift for making a yummy smoothie! Easy, fast and delish! In 2011, she revamped our Smoothie collection and took out super complicated recipes and replaced them with simple and fresh. I loved it and I know you will too!

Athena Juice

Degree of Difficulty: Easy

Supercharged with superfoods - wisdom and beauty will be yours with this powerful start to the day!

1 head romaine
1 cucumber, unpeeled
2 red apples
5 stalks celery
1 inch ginger
1/2 lemon

Procedure
Juice all ingredients, ideally in a twin gear juicer.

Review
It has a little bit of a sour kick to it. Very addictive!! - Audubon, NJ 2/10/2011

Brazil Nut Milk

Degree of Difficulty: Easy

Your raw alternative is good to that last drop. Best over cereal - hands down!

6 cups water
1 cup Brazil nuts
3 tablespoons agave nectar
1 teaspoon vanilla beans

Procedure
Blend all ingredients in Vitamix for 60 seconds. Strain through nut milk bag into large glass jar to remove the nut pulp.

Cacao Bean

Degree of Difficulty: Moderately difficult

Comparing it to hot chocolate makes the point but misses the heart-stirring perfection. Heated just enough, cacao bean is a smooth mug of Brazil Nut Milk doctored with banana, raw chocolate and maca, the latter a vitality booster. It both wraps you in fireside comfort and revs you up for the day.

2 cups almost boiling water
1 red banana or
1/2 half yellow banana
1/2 cup cashews
3 dates
3 heaping tablespoons cacao
1 heaping tablespoon maca

Brazil Nut Milk
2 cups water
1/3 cup Brazil nuts
1 tablespoon agave nectar
1/3 teaspoon vanilla beans

Procedure

1. Make Brazil Nut Milk. Separate 2 cups - store remaining amount for later use.
2. Blend 2 cups Brazil Nut Milk and all other ingredients except water.
3. Turn blender down to 3 on the Vitamix dial to avoid creating foam.
4. Slowly add hot water from spring water dispenser.
5. Mix slowly till water is incorporated.
6. Blend all ingredients in Vitamix for 60 seconds. Strain through nut milk bag into large glass jar to remove the nut pulp.

Review

Holy cow! This might be my favorite beverage in the world! Yum. It's simultaneously rich and delicate, super silky, chocolatey perfection. - KS

Out of all the Pure Market Express items we carry, this is my personal favorite. This is the one I pick as a post-workout recovery, as well as a morning wakeup on the days I don't have time to make something. Chocolate heaven - guilt-free! - S. Queen, New Freeport, PA

Nice chocolate smoothy - made a great milkshake. - JA Smith, Marcellus, MI 12/26/2012

Caribbean Blend Smoothie

Degree of Difficulty: Easy

Our own spin on a trip to the Caribbean, with oceans of orange and pineapple juice, strawberry umbrellas and peachy sands..

2 cups peaches, frozen
1 cup strawberries, frozen
2 oranges, juiced
1 small pineapple, juiced
1 banana

Procedure

1. Juice oranges and pineapple.
2. Blend juice and frozen fruit till smooth.

Chocolate Banana Smoothie

Degree of Difficulty: Easy

Chocolate and banana mixed to create this glass of chilled bliss..

3 bananas
1/2 cup agave nectar
3 tablespoons cacao powder
1/8 teaspoon vanilla beans
1/8 teaspoon sea salt

Brazil Nut Milk
6 cups water
1 cup Brazil nuts
3 tablespoons agave nectar
1 teaspoon vanilla beans

Procedure:

1. Make Brazil Nut Milk - separate 3 cups and add to blender. Store remaining Brazil Nut Milk for later use.
2. Blend 3 cups Brazil Nut Milk and all other ingredients.
3. Enjoy!

Classic Green Smoothie

Degree of Difficulty: Easy

Imagine consuming 4 cups of raw spinach upon waking. Sweetly masked by strawberries, bananas, Brazil Nut Milk and agave nectar, all that remains is the green plus oodles of iron, calcium, vitamins K and A and more. Good morning, indeed.

1 banana
1 cup strawberries, frozen
2 cups spinach, packed
2 dates

Brazil Nut Milk
4 cups water
2/3 cup Brazil nuts
2 tablespoons agave nectar
1/2 teaspoon vanilla beans

Procedure

1. Make Brazil Nut Milk.
2. Blend Brazil Nut Milk with all remaining ingredients until smooth.
3. Show off your green moustache!

Review

Confession time - I hate spinach...seriously...I know it's good for you, and so I hide it among other mixed greens and try to ignore it in my salad. But that doesn't amount to much spinach, and cooking it...ugh! That's even worse! Good news is - the only clue it's in this smoothie is the color; if healthy were always this tasty, we could solve the health crisis! Sweet, sweet success, Pure Market Express, you've made me a convert! I'm calling this smoothie "Spinach Redeemed!" - D. Landry, Lynwood, WA

Coconut Milk

Degree of Difficulty: Easy

Cool refreshing goodness anytime!

1 teaspoon vanilla beans
1/2 cup coconut meat

2 cups Coconut Water
1/4 teaspoon sea salt

Procedure

1. Blend all ingredients until smooth.
2. Strain through nut milk bag.

Cran Orange Splash

Degree of Difficulty: Easy

Cranberries and oranges form an unusual bond completed by sweet apples.

4 oranges, juiced
2 granny smith apples, juiced
1 cup cranberries

Procedure

1. Juice oranges and apples.
2. Blend juices with berries.
3. Slurp!

Creamy Strawberry Smoothie

Degree of Difficulty: Easy

With its sunshiny, strawberry-patch flavor and consistency of soft serve ice cream, our creamy strawberry smoothie rewards your a.m. awakening with a dessert-like treat. Add ice and whiz it through the blender for a nostalgic glass of strawberry milk.

3 cups strawberries, frozen
1 tablespoon lemon juice
1/2 avocado
2 dates

Brazil Nut Milk
2 cups water
1/3 cup Brazil nuts
1 tablespoons agave nectar
1/3 teaspoon vanilla beans

Procedure

1. Make Brazil Nut Milk - separate 4 cups and add to blender. Store remaining Brazil Nut Milk for later use.
2. Blend 4 cups of Brazil Nut Milk and all other ingredients until smooth.
3. Enjoy pink power!!

Drop of Sunshine Juice

Degree of Difficulty: Easy

A sweet combination of citrus and pineapple to start any day on the right foot.

4 oranges, juiced
1 grapefruit, juiced
1 pineapple, juiced

Procedure:

1. Juice all ingredients and combine.
2. Give the juice a whirl to combine and stick in a straw.

Fruit Fabulous-ity

Degree of Difficulty: Easy

Filled with tasty fruits, this smoothie is a fab way to start any day.

5 cups oranges, juiced
2 cups mangos, frozen
1 cup strawberries
1 cup peaches

Procedure
1. Juice oranges.
2. Add juice to all other ingredients and blend till smooth.
3. Enjoy!

Green Sweet Tart Juice

Degree of Difficulty: Easy

Taste travel back to the days of Sweet Tarts, those mouth-puckering candies of childhood. A whole lemon and lime tart up our juicy blend of celery, romaine, pineapple and apple, while carrot sweetens the affair. It's candy in a glass. Serve it frozen or chilled for extra perk.

6 stalks celery
4 granny smith apples
1 lemon
1 lime
1 pineapple
1 full 6 oz bag of spinach

Procedure
1. Juice all ingredients.
2. Pucker up and smile!

Review
I ordered the weekly smoothies/juices and this was the first one I tried. Excellent, I loved it! Was still a little frozen but that made it also kind of like a slushie treat. This is tart but not overly powering and the juice didn't have any gritty or pulpy texture to it. - Jennifer S., PA
Refreshing! Surprisingly refreshing...it does taste like the candy. Thanks for the memories! - AM Day, Baraboo, MI

Holiday Nog

Degree of Difficulty: Easy

6 cups water
1 cup Brazil nuts
2 bananas
3 dates
1 teaspoon cinnamon
1/8 teaspoon vanilla beans
1/8 teaspoon sea salt

Procedure
1. Blend water and Brazil nuts.
2. Strain through a nut milk bag.
3. Return to Vitamix and blend in the remaining ingredients.
4. Blend at least 45 seconds until smooth.

Lime Berry Smoothie

Degree of Difficulty: Easy

Sweet strawberries and raspberries, team up with fresh juiced limes to provide the perfect combination of sweet and tart.

2 cups red apples, juice only
2 cups strawberries, frozen
1/2 cup raspberries, frozen
1/4 cup lime juice

Procedure

1. Juice apples till you have 2 cups of juice.
2. Blend apple juice will all other ingredients till smooth.

Master Cleanse Lemonade

Degree of Difficulty: Easy

A classic cleanser - best first thing in the morning hot and spicy!

2 cups water, ideally hot
2 tablespoons lemon juice
1 tablespoon maple syrup
Cayenne to taste

Procedure

Blend all ingredients in blender.

Orange Mango Creamsicle

Degree of Difficulty: Easy

Three simple ingredients make this smoothie a perfect creamy masterpiece

6 oranges, juiced
1 cup mangos, frozen
1 tablespoon coconut butter

Procedure

1. Juice oranges.
2. Blend juice and all other ingredients together till smooth.

Pandora`s Peach Smoothie

Degree of Difficulty: Easy

A sweet combination of citrus and pineapple to start any day on the right foot.

4 oranges, juiced
1 grapefruit, juiced
1 pineapple, juiced
Brazil Nut Milk
6 cups water
1 cup Brazil nuts
3 tablespoons agave nectar
1 teaspoon vanilla beans

Procedure

1. Make Brazil Nut Milk - separate 2 cups and add to blender. Store remaining Brazil Nut Milk for later use.
2. Blend all ingredients until smooth.

Review

This is a favorite grab and go item - and the particular favorite of our stock manager, who always makes sure he's on hand when the shipment comes in, so he can "make sure they taste OK" before filling our freezer! - S. Queen, New Freeport, PA

Pecan Nog

Degree of Difficulty: Easy

Filled with tasty fruits, this smoothie's is a fab way to start any day.

5 cups water
1 cup pecans
1/2 cup maple syrup
3 tablespoons coconut butter
1/2 teaspoon vanilla beans
3/4 teaspoon cinnamon

Procedure

1. Blend pecans and water until smooth.
2. Strain through a nut milk bag.
3. Return milk to blend and blend in remaining ingredients.

POM Party

Degree of Difficulty: Easy

Pomegranate at its finest.

2 cups strawberries, frozen
2 cups peaches, frozen
1 banana
3 pomegranate juice
(can also use POM Juice)

Procedure

Blend

Review

Love this! This is a very tasty blend, the flavors harmonize perfectly. I added a touch of vanilla powder and, oh my, yumminess! - R. Guevara, Springfield, MO

Raspberry Smash Smoothie

Degree of Difficulty: Easy

Scrumptious raspberries are accompanied by strawberries, bananas and red apples in this chilled symphony.

4 red apples, juiced
2 cups strawberries, frozen
1 cup raspberries, frozen
1 banana

Procedure

1. Juice apples.
2. Blend juice with all other ingredients till smooth.

Razzle Smoothie

Degree of Difficulty: Easy

Dazzle your system with a rush of red: raspberries, apples and goji berries. Lovely enough to serve in a goblet yet bottled and ready for a morning commute, it's ready to please whenever and wherever.

2 cups frozen raspberries
1/2 avocado
2 tablespoons lemon juice
1 red apple, cored

Brazil Nut Milk
6 cups water
1 cup Brazil nuts
3 tablespoons agave nectar
1 teaspoon vanilla beans

Procedure

1. Make Brazil Nut Milk - separate 4 cups and add to blender. Store remaining Brazil Nut Milk for later use.
2. Blend Brazil Nut Milk with all other ingredients until smooth.

Review

Very satisfying. Tastes like raspberry sherbert but more flavorful and rich because of the other ingredients. Love it as an after dinner snack! - J. Kerrine, Silver Spring, MD

Ruby Red Sunrise

Degree of Difficulty: Easy

Cleansing beet with just the perfect amount of sweetness.

1 beet, medium
2 carrots
2 red apples
1/2 bunch parsley
2 oranges
2 granny smith apples

Procedure

1. Juice all and mix.
2. Could you be Betty Boop with those red lips?

Tahitian Treat Smoothie

Degree of Difficulty: Easy

Berry delights with a tag along pineapple to sweeten the deal.

1 cup strawberries, frozen
1/2 cup peaches, frozen
1/2 cup blueberries, frozen
1 pineapple, juiced

Procedure

1. Juice pineapple.
2. Blend pineapple juice and all other ingredients together till smooth.

Thin Mint Smoothie

Degree of Difficulty: Easy

All hail the former Girl Scout who invented this tall cool one! A devilish dessert as well, it's dark. It's chocolaty. It's minty. If this is healthful eating—and it most certainly is—you'll exclaim, "Sign me up!"

1 banana, frozen
3 tablespoons cacao powder
3-5 drops peppermint essential oil

Brazil Nut Milk
6 cups water
1 cup Brazil nuts
3 tablespoons agave nectar
1 teaspoon vanilla beans

Procedure

1. Make Brazil Nut Milk - separate 2 cups and add to blender. Store remaining Brazil Nut Milk for later use.
2. Blend all remaining ingredients with Brazil Nut Milk until smooth.
3. Listen to your inner Girl Scout shout with joy!

Review

Divine, rich chocolaty goodness in a glass. Though I didn't taste the mint, it was still GOOD TO THE LAST DROP! - AM Day, Baraboo, MI

Tropical Peach Smoothie

Degree of Difficulty: Easy

A delightful combo of pineapple, banana, orange and peach - YUM!

4 cups peaches, frozen
1 banana

2 oranges, juiced
1 pineapple, juiced

Procedure

Juice oranges and pineapple. Blend juice and other ingredients until smooth.

Soup

Spicy Cilantro

Tomato Herb

Corn Chowder

The truth comes out. I love Spicy Cilantro Soup and Tzatziki Soup as chip dips but I am really not a huge fan of soups in general. Watermelon Soup was created after we had some watermelon salsa once that I thought I would hate but ended up in love with. My husband, Quentin, was a big part of Tomato Herb Soup and Corn Chowder though I confess I am a fan of the Corn Chowder straight out of a warm saucepan on a Minnesota winter day.

Corn Chowder

Degree of Difficulty: Easy

Rich, creamy, chunky: All the choice chowder adjectives apply! Fresh-from-the-cob kernels take up residency in a walnut-garlic based enriched with olive oil. Warm slightly for the comfort-food effect.

3 cups corn, fresh or frozen
1/2 cup walnuts
1/2 avocado
1/2 cup red onions
1/4 cup extra virgin olive oil
2 cloves garlic
1 teaspoon black pepper
2 cups water, more as needed to desired consistency
1/4 cup cilantro

Bac'Un
1 eggplant, peeled and cut into 1.5 mm slices
1/4 cup ume plum vinegar
1/4 cup extra virgin olive oil
1/8 teaspoon cayenne

Procedure
Make the Bac'Un:
1. Peel the eggplant. Slice with a mandolin at 1.5 mm.
2. Marinate eggplant slices with ume plum vinegar, extra virgin olive oil and cayenne for at least one hour.
3. Lay slices flat on teflex and dehydrate at 105 degrees for 12 hours or until crispy.
4. Rough chop 1 cup of Bac'Un. Remaining Bac'Un can be stored on the countertop in an airtight container.

Make Da Soup:
1. Blend all ingredients together EXCEPT Bac'Un, cilantro and 1 cup corn. Pour into a serving dish.
2. Mix Bac'Un, cilantro and remaining corn in a separate bowl. Add this mixture as a soup topping.
3. Warm if desired in dehydrator or saucepan until warm to the touch.

Spicy Cilantro Soup

Degree of Difficulty: Easy

There's no greener green on our menu and it's little wonder: Spinach, cilantro avocado, lime and jalapeño compose this creamy delight. Pair with our Corn Chips & Salsa for a picture- and palate-perfect main meal.

3 cups water
1 bag fresh spinach (6 oz)
1/2 cup coconut meat
1/2 cup cilantro, minced
1/2 avocado
1 tablespoon tamari
2 tablespoons lime juice

Procedure
Blend all ingredients until smooth.

Tomato Herb Soup

Degree of Difficulty: Easy

A smoothly pureed soup that's tomato times two: We use fresh as well as sun-dried for depth of flavor, accenting the pair with garlic and gingerroot for edge and olive oil for richness.

3 cups tomatoes
1 cup sun-dried tomatoes, soaked
1 cup water
1/2 cup avocado
1/2 cup yellow onions
1/2 cup extra virgin olive oil
2 cloves garlic
1 tablespoon lemon juice
1/2 teaspoon black pepper
1/2 inch ginger root
1/2 jalapeño pepper, seeded

Procedure
Blend all ingredients until smooth.

Tzatziki Soup

Degree of Difficulty: Easy

The classic Greek sauce finds its way into a soup bowl. Cool cucumber, of course, stars, but we inventively replace traditional yogurt with an avocado-onion blend. Fresh dill and parsley contribute perk.

2 cups water
1/2 cucumber
1 stalk celery
1/2 avocado
1/2 cup parsley, chopped
1/4 cup red onions
2 cloves garlic
1 tablespoon dill
Salt and freshly ground black pepper to taste

Procedure
Blend all ingredients until smooth.

Review
Nice blend of flavors, very true to what I think of as tzatziki, but mild so I added additional seasoning myself. Would like stronger flavor. It's very good, just amp it up! - Stephanie, Apple Valley, MN

Watermelon Soup

Degree of Difficulty: Easy

A summery soup for anytime, our watermelon mélange stars lime, mint, ginger, honey and cardamom. Mango chunks makes it less a sipper than a spooner. A pleasantly light lunch or elegant dinnertime first course.

4 cups watermelon
2 cups of seasonal fruit or mangos
1/4 cup lime juice
3 tablespoons mint
1 tablespoon minced ginger root
1 tablespoon honey
1/8 teaspoon cardamom

Procedure

1. Place 3 cups watermelon and 1 cup mangos or diced seasonal fruit in Vitamix and blend until smooth.
2. Ball up the remaining 1 cup watermelon and 1 cup mangos or diced seasonal fruit with melon baller and fold into the puree.
3. Separately blend the lime juice, mint, ginger, honey and cardamom.
4. Fold into soup and dig in.

Review

Really liked the flavors in this soup. My order came with watermelon balls and raspberries that I added to the soup. Just great! - Stephanie, Apple Valley, MN
This wasn't just some watermelon thrown in a blender, it had ginger and other spices and fruit that made it really flavorful. If it weren't for the chunks of fruit slowing me down (mine had strawberries), I would have just guzzled it down. - Tanya, Newport, MN
I will never make watermelon soup again. This soup is by far my favorite item from PME. I plan to use this soup as a refreshing part of my cleanse. Perfect balance of melon, mango and spice. YUM! - AM Day, Baraboo, MI

Banana Cream Pie

Desserts

Chocolate Ice Cream

Caramel Macaroons

YUM-mazing Desserts

Ahhh this is where I live! I L-O-V-E dessert! These are the ones that everyone agreed were the best of the best when we launched Pure Market Express. I tend to make a whole ton of desserts and then freeze them. That way I can chunk off just the right piece when I am craving something yummy.

Honestly, I believe that dessert is the gateway drug to healthy eating. If you can convince the average SAD diet consumer that a healthy dessert is just as good and craveworthy as the usual stuff, we could revolutionize the health of our country. If dessert is good, I might give a side dish a shot. Maybe an entrée and so on. I challenge you all to take one of these recipes to your next family get together, don't tell anyone it's healthy and watch it disappear.

The fact is that food, real food, tastes better than anything that ever came out of a factory – we just need to remind ourselves how good it really is.

Almond Bliss

Degree of Difficulty: Easy

Chocolate-y pieces of heaven are Pure Markets answer to the Almond Joy

1 cup coconut butter
1/2 cup cacao powder
1/2 cup agave nectar
1 cup shredded coconut
1 cup whole almonds

Procedure

1. Blend agave, coconut butter, and cacao in blender until incorporated. Should be thick like cold molasses.
2. Before beginning assembly, put on rubber gloves with a small amount of coconut oil rubbed on them.
3. Place 1 teaspoon chocolate mixture on the palm of your hand and spread gently to about the size of a silver dollar.
4. Place 1 whole almond in the center and wrap the chocolate around it.
5. Roll the chocolate almond in coconut.
6. Repeat until you run out of chocolate.
7. Let set for 30-60 min in the fridge if you can. ;0)

Review

These chocolate covered almonds (rolled in coconut) are delicious. They are so rich that only one is enough and unlike some raw chocolates, the chocolate is creamy, not too dense. - Angela, NY

Banana Cream Pie

Degree of Difficulty: Easy

You'll go both nuts and bananas over this lush spin on the classic. Ideal for breakfast (it's bananas, after all!) and always perfect as dessert, ours sits atop a sweetened almond crust and credits its sweetness to a drizzle of agave.

Crust:
2 cups almonds
1/8 cup agave nectar

Filling:
6 bananas
2 cups Young Thai coconut meat
1/2 cup agave nectar
1/2 cup coconut butter
1/4 teaspoon vanilla beans
water, just enough to move the blender blades

Procedure

Make the Crust

1. In a food processor, process almonds and agave roughly for crust.
2. Gently press crust mixture into the bottom of a 9-inch pie pan

Make the Pie

1. Slice 4 bananas thinly into rounds. Layer them neatly on your completed crust.
2. In Vitamix, blend remaining 2 bananas and all other filling ingredients EXCEPT coconut butter until completely smooth.
3. Then slowly add coconut butter until completely incorporated & smooth.
4. Add water if needed to keep the blender blades moving. Finished filling should be slightly thicker than buttermilk.
5. Pour filling on top of layered bananas
6. Freeze for at least 1 hour to set or refrigerate overnight. Serve.

Review

Thought this was phenomenal. Creamy, flavorful, satisfying. Will be ordering this one again. - Stephanie, Apple Valley, MN

This pie has a great texture and authentic banana flavor. It is sweet but not TOO sweet and not overly heavy like some raw pies that rely too heavily on avocado or other high-fat elements. The crunchy almond bits really balance out the texture. One PME portion actually is about 2 very satisfying servings for me. This pie is a lovely fluffy treat - you will not be disappointed! - Kristina, Bay Area, CA

The banana cream pie is the first breakfast that I have tried from PME. I was blown away! This is also the first dish that I tried from PME. I used to be a meat lover, and only recently turned to eating raw for health benefits and I have to say that I have had good and bad experiences with raw prepared food. This one did NOT disappoint. It all the more convinced me that eating raw does not mean having to suffer on flavor and still being able to enjoy food. I am super happy I found PME! - Karla, NY

Bliss Balls

Degree of Difficulty: Easy

Cacao nibs, goji berries and more mold together with hemp seeds to form a distinct texture and decadent reward. It doesn't get any better than this!

1 cup goji berries
1 cup hemp seeds
1 cup coconut butter
1/2 cup cacao nibs
1/2 cup cacao
2 tablespoons agave nectar
1/2 teaspoon vanilla beans
1/8 teaspoon sea salt

Procedure

1. Add all ingredients to a food processor. Process until the goji berries are completely broken down into small pieces, with all pieces uniform in size.
2. Hand roll 1 tablespoon of the goji berry mixture with gloved hands. Squeeze firmly to get every yummy ingredient stuck together.

Reviews

These are appropriately named! Had a hard time sharing these because they were so good. - Stephanie, Apple Valley, MN 9/4/2009
I plan to eat a few every day. Not only do they satisfy my sweet tooth like nothing before, they make me happy!! - Brunswick, GA 2/26/2011
They taste like a raw dark chocolate dessert to me. I'm always looking for something more "traditional." For the hardcore raw peeps this might be a five star for you.
- L. Cullen, Village Mills, TX 8/3/2012

C4 (aka Chocolate Chocolate Chip Cookies)

Degree of Difficulty: Moderately difficult

So it's overkill on the chocolate! Any chocoholic understands and will be in sweet heaven.

2 cups oat groats, ground to flour
1-1/2 cups maple syrup
1 cup cashews, ground to flour
1 cup cacao
1/2 cup water
1 tablespoon vanilla beans
1 teaspoon sea salt

Chocolate Chips
1 cup cashews, soaked
3/4 cup maple syrup
1/2 cup cacao
1/4 teaspoon vanilla beans
1/4 teaspoon sea salt
water as needed to loosen while blending

Procedure

1. Grind oat groats in the Wonder Mill.
2. Grind cashews in blender in 1 cup portions to prevent making butter.
3. Place all ingredients in mixer with a dough hook and mix until it becomes a rollable dough.
4. Roll out dough to 1/4 inch thick and cut cookies shapes with 3 1/8 round cut.
5. Make Chocolate Chip batter.
6. Blend all ingredients until smooth
7. Pipe on 6 chocolate chips per cookies.
8. Dehydrate for 8-12 hours or overnight at 105 degrees.

Recipe Tips

** Extra Chocolate Chip batter can be piped directly onto teflex sheets and dehydrated for 24 hours at 105 degrees. Then freeze them and you'll have yum-mazingly healthy chocolate chips any time you feel a craving coming on.

Reviews

From the first bite, I said wow, this is really good. It has a cake-like texture and a nice chocolate flavor. The chocolate chips on top look perfect. I got more cookies than I expected. I will be ordering these again. - V. Tow, Placerville, CA
What's not to like about double chocolate cookies? Moist and delicious - JA Smith, Marcellus, MI

Caramel Macaroons

Degree of Difficulty: Easy

With your coffee in the morning or with your wine at night - either way these are perfect!

2 cups shredded coconut
1/2 cup dates, soaked
1/4 cup coconut butter
1/4 cup agave nectar
1 teaspoon cinnamon

Procedure

1. Place dates (soaked if not soft), butter, agave and cinnamon in food processor and process till smooth to make the caramel.
2. Hand mix coconut and date mixture.
3. Scoop on teflex sheets with small ice cream scoop.
4. Dehydrate until crisp outside and soft inside, about 4 hours and no more than 12 at 105 degrees.

Recipe Tips

** When you're feeling adventurous, try using a tablespoon of lucuma instead of dates. It is a completely different caramel, almost like milk caramel.
**The Incan superfood lucuma powder features a full-bodied caramel taste plus an all-star nutrient lineup of beta-carotene, niacin and iron.

Cherry Chocolate Chip Ice Cream

Degree of Difficulty: Easy

This is my favorite ice cream - hands down!

Ice Cream Base:
3 cups water
1/2 cup Brazil nuts
1 red banana or 1/2 half yellow banana
2 dates
1/8 teaspoon sea salt

Cra-mazing Flavor:
4 cups cherries, frozen
2 cups agave nectar
1 avocado, over-ripe
1/2 cup coconut butter
1 teaspoon vanilla beans

Chocolate Chips
1 cup cashews, soaked
3/4 cup maple syrup
1/2 cup cacao
1/2 teaspoon sea salt
1/4 teaspoon vanilla beans
water as needed to loosen while blending

Procedure

Make the Chocolate Chips

1. Make the chocolate chip batter by blending all ingredients until smooth.
2. Pipe directly onto teflex and dehydrate for 24 hours at 105 degrees.

Make the Ice Cream

1. Rough chop cherries. If frozen, allow to thaw at least halfway before using.
2. Blend ice cream base for at least 60 second in the Vitamix. Strain through nut milk bag.
3. Return base to blender carafe and add agave, avocado coconut butter and 1 cup cherries and blend until smooth.
4. If you have an ice cream maker, put your ice cream base in the ice cream maker.
5. When cycle is 3/4 way done, add remaining cherries and chocolate chips.
6. If you DON'T have an ice cream maker, fold cherries and chocolate chips gently into ice cream mixture.
7. Freeze for at least 24 hours.

Chocolate Chip Cookies

Degree of Difficulty: Easy

A classic favorite with a raw twist. Cashews, oats and cacao nibs packaged into 8 monster big cookies. These are more than just your grandma's cookies.

2 cups cashews
1 cup oat groats, measure then grind
3 tablespoons agave nectar
3 tablespoons coconut oil
1/8 teaspoon vanilla beans

Chocolate Chips
1 cup cashews, soaked
3/4 cup maple syrup
1/2 cup cacao
1/4 teaspoon vanilla beans
1/4 teaspoon sea salt
water as needed to loosen while blending

Procedure

1. Make the chocolate chip batter by blending all ingredients until smooth.
2. Pipe directly onto to teflex and dehydrate for 24 hours at 105 degrees.
3. Grind oat groats to flour, ideally in a grain mill such as a Wonder Mill but this can also be done in a Vitamix.
4. Process cashews in blender to make cashew flour.
5. Mix all ingredients by hand. Make sure the cashews are very finely ground.
6. Fold in 1/2 cup chocolate chips. Freeze the rest to have on hand for future goodies.
7. Scoop dough with large ice cream scoop and flatten. Cool in refrigerator.

Reviews

I wasn't really sure what to expect when I purchased the chocolate chip cookies but I really enjoyed them. I was surprised at how big they were and how many I got for the price. I am going to try the chocolate chocolate chip next. Definitely worth the money. - Antioch, TN
Whoooah!! These are goooood! - Raw Seeker
We enjoyed these so much - best raw cookies - JA Smith, Marcellus, MI

Chocolate Ice Cream

Degree of Difficulty: Easy

What can we say? Healthy chocolate ice cream that tastes CRA-MAZING!!

Ice Cream Base:
3 cups water
1/2 cup Brazil nuts
1 red banana or 1/2 half yellow banana
1/4 teaspoon cinnamon
1/8 teaspoon vanilla beans
1/8 teaspoon sea salt
2 dates

Cra-mazing Flavor:
1/2 cup coconut butter
2 cup agave nectar
2 avocados, over-ripe
1 cup cacao

Procedure

1. Blend ice cream base for at least 60 seconds in a Vitamix.
2. Strain base through nut milk bag.
3. Blend ice cream base with all other ingredients until smooth.
4. Place in ice cream maker and freeze until it reaches soft serve consistency.

Recipe Tips

** If you don't have an ice cream maker, you can simply freeze it straight out of the blender. The ice cream maker will give you a smoother finished texture with less ice crystals. However, a straight freeze is JUST as yummy!

Chocolate Macaroons

Degree of Difficulty: Easy

This beloved cookie is packed full of cacao, maple syrup and coconut. Crisp on the outside, soft on the inside and "Mmm" all around.

3 cups shredded coconut
1/2 cup cacao
3/4 cup maple syrup
1/3 cup coconut butter
1/4 teaspoon vanilla bean
1/8 teaspoon sea salt

Procedure

1. Blend cacao, maple syrup, vanilla, and salt until smooth, then add coconut butter and blend until smooth.
2. Add liquid to the shredded coconut in a mixing bowl.
3. Mix with gloved hands until sticky dough is achieved.
4. Scoop on teflex sheets with small ice cream scoop or melon baller.
5. Dehydrate until crisp outside and soft inside, about 4 hours and no more than 12 at 105 degrees.

Cookie Dough Ice Cream

Degree of Difficulty: Easy

Ben? Jerry? Who are they? MMMM-good.

Ice Cream Base:
3 cups water
1/2 cup Brazil nuts
1 red banana or 1/2 half yellow banana
2 dates
1/4 teaspoon cinnamon
1/8 teaspoon sea salt

Cra-mazing Flavor:
2 cups agave nectar
2 avocados, over ripe
1/2 cup coconut butter
1 teaspoon vanilla beans
1/2 recipe Chocolate Chip Cookies

Procedure

1. Blend ice cream base for at least 60 seconds in a Vitamix.
2. Strain base through nut milk bag.
3. Blend ice cream base with all other ingredients until smooth.
4. Place in ice cream maker and freeze until it reaches soft serve consistency.
5. Dice Chocolate Chip cookies and fold in until you see cookies with every turn of the spoon.

Recipe Tips

** If you don't have an ice cream maker, you can simply freeze it straight out of the blender. The ice cream maker will give you a smoother finished texture with less ice crystals. However, a straight freeze is JUST as yummy!

French Vanilla Ice Cream

Degree of Difficulty: Easy

No plain ol' vanilla here - this a rich comforting french vanilla that just cries out for fresh strawberries!

Ice Cream Base:
3 cups water
1/2 cup Brazil nuts
1 red banana or 1/2 half yellow banana
2 dates
1/8 teaspoon cinnamon
1/8 teaspoon sea salt

Cra-mazing Flavor:
2 cups agave nectar
2 avocados, over ripe
1/2 cup coconut butter
2 teaspoons vanilla beans

Procedure

1. Blend ice cream base for at least 60 seconds in a Vitamix.
2. Strain base through nut milk bag.
3. Blend ice cream base with all other ingredients until smooth.
4. Place in ice cream maker and freeze until it reaches soft serve consistency.

Recipe Tips

** If you don't have an ice cream maker, you can simply freeze it straight out of the blender. The ice cream maker will give you a smoother finished texture with less ice crystals. However, a straight freeze is JUST as yummy!

No Bake Cookies

Degree of Difficulty: Easy

Peanut butter cookies, meet oatmeal cookies. Nutty almond butter, sweet maple syrup and an infusion of cacao powder make these oatmeal discs irresistible.

3 cups rolled oats
3/4 cup maple syrup
3/4 cup almond butter
3 tablespoons cacao
1 tablespoon water
1 teaspoon coconut oil
1/2 teaspoon vanilla beans

Procedure

1. In a food processor, process all ingredients EXCEPT rolled oats until completely smooth.
2. Mix rolled oats in by hand until you have a pretty thick dough.
3. Place on dehy teflex sheet, one small level ice cream scoop flattened.
4. Dehydrate until dry but still soft and flexible, 12-24 hours at 105 degrees.
5. Gnosh immediately or store in an air container in the freezer or refrigerator.

Maple Ice Cream

Degree of Difficulty: Easy

Maple yum - or add some Texas pecans and make it Maple Nut!

Ice Cream Base:
3 cups water
1/2 cup Brazil nuts
1 red banana or 1/2 half yellow banana
1/4 teaspoon cinnamon
1/8 teaspoon sea salt
2 dates

Cra-mazing Flavor:
1-1/2 cups maple syrup
1 avocado, over-ripe
1/2 cup coconut butter
1/8 teaspoon vanilla beans

Procedure

1. Blend ice cream base for at least 60 seconds in a Vitamix.
2. Strain base through nut milk bag.
3. Blend ice cream base with all other ingredients until smooth.
4. Place in ice cream maker and freeze until it reaches soft serve consistency.

Recipe Tips

** If you don't have an ice cream maker, you can simply freeze it straight out of the blender. The ice cream maker will give you a smoother finished texture with less ice crystals. However, a straight freeze is JUST as yummy!

Pecan Pie

Degree of Difficulty: Moderately difficult

Healthy has NEVER tasted this good!

Candied Pecans:
4 cups pecans
1 cup agave nectar
1/2 teaspoon sea salt

Crust:
4 cups pecans, divided
3-1/2 cups oat groats
1 cup water
3/4 cup cashews
1/3 cup maple syrup
1/3 cup agave nectar
1/8 teaspoon vanilla beans

Pecan Filling:
15 dates, soaked
1 cup cashews
1 cup water
1 cup maple syrup
1/3 cup coconut butter
1 tablespoon Irish moss, soaked
1 teaspoon cinnamon
1/8 teaspoon sea salt

Procedure

For candied pecans

1. Rough Chop Pecans in food processor.
2. Soak 4 cups pecans in warm water for at least one hour.
3. Toss with 1 cup agave and dehydrate at 118 degrees.

For Crust

1. Grind oat groats in Wonderrmill till you have 3.5 cups of flour, approx 2 cups groats.
2. Put 3 cups pecans in the food processor. Process until the nuts start release oil and create butter. May have to scrape down sides several times.
3. Process 1 cup pecans, water, cashews, maple syrup, agave, sea salt and vanilla bean until smooth in food processor.
4. Then add pecan butter and process again.
5. Slowly add oat groat flour until you have a firm dough until a ball of dough forms around the food processor blades.
6. Press crust into a 9-inch pie pan.
7. Refrigerate finished crust.

For Filling

1. Soak Irish moss in one cup hot water. Set aside.
2. Blend all remaining ingredients together until smooth.
3. Drain and rinse Irish moss thoroughly
4. Remove candied pecans from dehydrator
5. Fold in 2 cups candied pecans. Set filling aside.

To Assemble:

1. Remove pie crust from refrigerator.
2. Pour in filling.
3. Top with neatly layered pecans.

Pecan Pie Truffles

Degree of Difficulty: Easy

What could make Pecan Pie better? Chocolate of course! Caramel pecans dipped in rich raw chocolate ready to pop!

2 cups pecans, pieces

The Caramel:
1/2 cup dates, soaked
1/2 cup coconut butter
1/4 cup agave nectar
1/2 teaspoon cinnamon

The Chocolate:
1/2 cup coconut oil
1/4 cup cacao powder
2 tablespoons agave nectar

Procedure

Rough chop pecan in food processor. Set aside.

Make the Caramel

1. Blend caramel ingredients until smooth.
2. Fold into chopped pecans until well covered.
3. Scoop onto teflex tray with small ice cream scoop.
4. Place in freezer for at least 30 minutes.

Dipping Chocolate

1. Coconut oil MUST be melted.
2. Place liquid oil in Vitamix. Start blender on low.
3. Slowly add cacao until well mixed, increasing speed to medium.
4. Finally drizzle in agave.

Assemble the Radical Goodness

1. Remove truffles from freezer.
2. Using tongs, dip into chocolate and set back on tray to firm.

Recipe Tips

** We used the tongs that come in a box of dates like you might get at Costco. You could also use regular household tongs.
** If you don't have tongs, you could carefully set the truffle on a fork and dip.
** Dipping must be done quickly as the chocolate will begin to set as soon as it begins to cool.

Review

All I can say is WOW! They taste like chocolate covered caramel candy, I'd never know they were raw! - Audubon, NJ
6 STARS! These are the best little treats - our family loves these little candies - JA Smith, Marcellus, MI

Strawberry Ice Cream

Degree of Difficulty: Easy

Springtime, robins, children playing and strawberry ice cream - oh yeah and its guilt-free too!

Ice Cream Base:
3 cups water
1/2 cup Brazil nuts
1 red banana or 1/2 half yellow banana
2 dates
1/8 teaspoon sea salt

Cra-mazing Flavor:
4 cups strawberries
2 cups agave nectar
2 avocados, over-ripe
1/2 cup coconut butter
1 teaspoon vanilla beans

Procedure

1. Rough chop strawberries; if frozen allow to thaw at least halfway before using.
2. Blend ice cream base for at least 60 second in the Vitamix. Strain through nut milk bag.
3. Return base to blender carafe and add agave, avocado coconut butter and one cup strawberries and blend until smooth.
4. If you have an ice cream maker, put your ice cream base in the ice cream maker.
5. When cycle is 3/4 way done, add remaining strawberries.
6. If you DON'T have an ice cream maker, fold strawberries gently into ice cream mixture.
7. Freeze for at least 24 hours.

Vanilla Macaroons

Degree of Difficulty: Easy

Same great flavor as our chocolate macaroons, only sans cacao and with a delicious introduction of nut pulp.

3 cups coconut, shredded
1 cup maple syrup
3/4 cup coconut butter
1 tablespoon vanilla extract
1-1/2 cups Brazil nut milk flour dehydrated from pulp leftover from milk

Procedure

1. Process desiccated coconut in food processor if it is NOT fine flake. Process until fine flake is achieved.
2. Process Brazil nuts to fine flour or use dehydrated pulp leftover from making Brazil Nut Milk
3. Mix coconut and nut pulp in bowl until evenly incorporated.
4. Blend maple syrup, coconut butter, and vanilla until smooth in Vitamix.
5. Mix with dry ingredients with gloved hands until sticky dough is achieved. DO NOT USE THE MIXER
6. Scoop on teflex sheets with small ice cream scoop.
7. Dehydrate until crisp outside and soft inside, about 4 hours and no more than 12 at 105 degrees.

Strawberry Shortcake

Degree of Difficulty: Moderately difficult

It's love by the layer: springy cake, creamy filling, sliced fresh strawberries, repeat, swoon. Pretty enough for a patisserie's glass case, our take on shortcake is entirely sans refined sugar, wheat and dairy.

The Cake:
4 cups strawberries, frozen
4 cups almonds, ground to flour
1 cup dates, soaked
1/2 cup coconut butter
2 tablespoons lemon juice
1/4 teaspoon vanilla beans
1/4 teaspoon sea salt

Whipped Cream:
1 cup cashews, soaked
2 cups Coconut Milk
1 cup coconut butter
1/2 cup agave nectar
1 tablespoon lemon juice
1/4 teaspoon vanilla beans
1/8 teaspoon sea salt

Procedure

1. Put frozen strawberries in a bowl to thaw.
2. Blend one cup Young Thai coconut meat with 2 cups milk to make coconut milk.

Make Whipped Cream

1. Add all ingredients to the Vitamix except the coconut butter and blend until smooth.
2. Slowly add coconut butter and blend until well incorporated.
3. Pour into a bowl and chill in refrigerator while making the cake.

Make the Cake

1. Make almond flour. Add 1 cup of almonds at a time to Vitamix and process slowly.
2. Sift flour if desired.
3. Combine all cake ingredients with almond flour and mix with hands. Should be a thick cake dough.
4. Form into 3 equal portions
5. Rough chop thawed berries in a food processor, should still be slightly chunky.

Assembly in an 8-inch Square Cake Pan

1. Layer 1/3 of the cake.
2. Then layer 1/2 of berry mixture.
3. Follow with 1/3 of cake dough.
4. Spread remaining half of berries.
5. Top with last 1/3 cup cake
6. Finally drizzle whipped cream and spread evenly over the top. Cream should work its way down the crevices of the cake to soak through the entire assembly.
7. Refrigerate overnight to set

Reviews

New to Raw I bought this for myself, the rest of the house is still on the SAD diet. So it was for ME but I shared a forkful with 2 family members and ate the rest. They were really disappointed to learn I ate the rest. It was delish!! I did add some more fresh strawberries to the top.
- Ivybox, Valparaiso, IN

Wonderful strawberry cake - lovely reminder of summer - JA Smith, Marcellus, MI

Pretty good. I like the crust the best! I will buy it again at some point, though my heart is with the lemon tart. - C. Paluch, Minneapolis, MN

Table Of Contents

HOW I GOT FAT & HOW PIE CHANGED EVERYTHING......5
EQUIPMENT LIST......11

Breakfast

Banana Breakfast Crepes......14
Cherry Honey Crunch Bars......15
Cinnamon Rolls......16
Cocogurt......17
Count Rawcula......17
Donut Holes......18
French Toast Oatmeal......19
Maple Apple Crepes......19
Pancakes......20
Strawberry Crunch......21
Tennessee Grawnola......21

Crackers, Chips & Cereal

Snacks and crackers!......24
Butter Walnut Bread......24
Chili Lime Crackers......25
Corn Chips......26
Garlic Crackers......27
Goji Trail Mix......27
Italian Flax......28
Onion Bread......29
Pepperoni Bites......30
Pizza Chips aka Tostada......31
Spicy Pepitas......31

Entrees

Bac`Un Burgers......33
Bac`Un Jalapeño Poppers......34
Baked Mac-n-Cheese Pasta......35
Basil Fried Rice Recipe......36
Big Greek Salad......37
Broccoli Salad......37
Caesar Salad......38
Chipotle Corn......38
Creamy Garlic 39
Dill Pasta......39
Fiesta Tostadas......40
Julie's Sushi......41
Lasagna......42
Manicotti......42
Mariachi Beet Wrap......44
Mexi Wrap......45
Pad Thai......46
Pasta Bolognese......47
Pepperoni Pizza......48
Pineapple Slaw......49
Pineapple Sweet & Sour......50
Quinoa Tabouli......51
Ravioli......52
Red Pepper Corn Salsa......53
Salmon & Hollandaise......54
Sausage Pizza......55
Spanish Rice......56
Spicy Peanut Pasta......57
Stir Fry-less......57
Taco Salad......58
Thai Salad......58
Turkey Salad Wrap......58

Nuts to the Good Cheese

Cheddar Cheese......60
Chipotle Garlic Cheese......61
Cilantro Jalapeño Cheese......61
Creamy Herb Cheese......62
Good as Gouda Cheese......63
Mexi Cheese......64
PepperJack Cheese......65
Simply Basil Cheese......66
Spicy Peppercorn Cheese......67
Tomato Basil Cheese......68

Seriously Good Components

Bac'Un......70
Hummus......70
Ketchup......70
Sassy Salsa......71
Sausage......71
Sour Cream......72
Spicy Lentil Taco Meat......72

Drinks

Athena Juice......74
Brazil Nut Milk......74
Cacao Bean.....75
Caribbean Blend Smoothie.....75
Chocolate Banana Smoothie......76
Classic Green Smoothie.....76
Coconut Milk.....76
Cran Orange Splash......77

Creamy Strawberry Smoothie......77
Drop of Sunshine Juice......77
Fruit Fabulous-ity......78
Green Sweet Tart Juice......78
Holiday Nog......78
Lime Berry Smoothie......79
Master Cleanse Lemonade......79
Orange Mango Creamsicle......79
Pandora`s Peach Smoothie......79
Pecan Nog......80
POM Party......80
Raspberry Smash Smoothie......80
Razzle Smoothie......81
Ruby Red Sunrise......81
Tahitian Treat Smoothie......81
Thin Mint Smoothie......82
Tropical Peach Smoothie......82
Tahitian Treat Smoothie......81
Thin Mint Smoothie......82
Tropical Peach Smoothie......82

Soup

Corn Chowder......84
Spicy Cilantro Soup......85
Tomato Herb Soup......85
Tzatziki Soup......85
Watermelon Soup......86

Desserts

YUM-mazing Desserts......88
Almond Bliss......88
Banana Cream Pie......89
Bliss Balls......90
C4 (aka Chocolate Chocolate Chip Cookies)......91
Caramel Macaroons......91
Cherry Chocolate Chip Ice Cream......92
Chocolate Chip Cookies......93
Chocolate Ice Cream......93
Chocolate Macaroons......94
Cookie Dough Ice Cream......94
French Vanilla Ice Cream......95
No Bake Cookies......95
Maple Ice Cream......96
Pecan Pie......97
Pecan Pie Truffles......98
Strawberry Ice Cream......99
Vanilla Macaroons......99
Strawberry Shortcake.....100

Pure Market Express was a spearhead raw vegan food delivery that was the inspiration and passion of Executive *Chef Rebecca Irey*. In four short years, they delivered thousands of breakfasts, lunches, dinners and desserts to health-conscious customers around the globe. Their desserts were picked up by grocery stores and at their peak were carried in over 550 stores around the United States.

A service ahead of their time, Pure Market Express was only able to serve their customers for a season but the passion behind the food lives on.

Now the recipes that inspired the movement can be yours! Dive in and start your own journey to radiant health today!

Pepperoni bites (page 30)

Maple Ice Cream (page 95)

Pad Thai (page 46)